The Debt Slayers

A Quick Guide for Slaying Debt and Living A More Fulfilling Life

Timothy & Dr. LeAnn Norris

The Debt Slayers

Published by Cultivate Freedom and Legacy LLC, Atlanta, Georgia.

Copyright © 2020 by Timothy Norris

FIRST EDITION

Book Design by Angela L. Walker

Interior Design by LeAnn Norris

Headshot Photos by Elle Wood

Edited by Jason Brown

thedebtslayers.com

ISBN 978-0-578-49871-3 (paperback)

Printed in the United States of America

CONTENTS

Introduction 1

PART 1: OUR STORY OF BECOMING DEBT SLAYERS

Chapter 1: The Honeymoon is Over 8

Chapter 2: The Middle-Class Squeeze 10

Chapter 3: Instant Gratification 15

Chapter 4: Enough is Enough 20

Chapter 5: Taking Action 24

Chapter 6: What Happened To Our Tesla? 28

Chapter 7: Consolidating Our Debt 31

Chapter 8: Becoming Debt Slayers 33

PART 2: LIVING A MORE FULFILLING LIFE

Chapter 9: Why Get Out of Debt? 52

Chapter 10: Frugality and Budgeting 59

Chapter 11: Minimize Your Life 69

PART 3: THE TOOLKIT FOR SLAYING DEBT

Chapter 12: Virtues of a Debt Slayer 76

Chapter 13: The 30+ Side Hustles Of A Debt Slayer 82

Chapter 14: The Debt Slayers Checklist 93

Definitions 99

Resources 104

Acknowledgements 105

About The Authors 106

Notes 108

INTRODUCTION

The Debt Slayers is not what you are thinking. This book is not about credit repair or how to leverage a credit score just to go deeper into debt. This is not a get-rich-quick idea book nor a financial book that will tell you how to invest your money or what mutual funds provide the highest return. Instead, this is a lifestyle book. A book about how to live, not financial advisory. Precisely, *The Debt Slayers* is a quick guide for slaying debt and living a more fulfilling life driven by lifestyle change. We discovered through our intense four-year journey of paying off $429,452.51 in debt, including anything from credit cards to student loans, that paying off your debt requires drastic behavior modification rooted in a lifestyle change. It also takes specific attributes to maintain these lifestyles.

Let us break it down. Your lifestyle determines what activities, interests, values, and allocations of income are essential in the world you live in. As a result, the lifestyle you choose will invariably influence your finances. When your lifestyle contradicts your financial goals, your behavior toward achieving those goals will surely contrast as well. For example, living luxuriously when in a mountain of debt will lead you to purchase things like the newest iPhone with all the bells and whistles instead of debt snowballing that one-off bonus check. This lifestyle and financial goal contradiction are a problem and a common dilemma with getting out of debt. This was an issue for our household too. There is good news though. We eventually wised up and figured out the lifestyle recipe of frugality and minimalism to clear all our debt in a timely manner. This book will walk you through the most pivotal ways of living to achieve total debt cancelation and provide a checklist with specific steps, ultimately for a more financially free and fulfilling life.

Please do not worry. We promise this won't be a fluffy book that merely gives hope through high-level lifestyle concepts. Instead, we will share our raw story of how we became debt slayers. Throughout the book, there will be dual narration where we each discuss various aspects of our road to becoming debt slayers. Hopefully, the dual narrative from chapter to chapter will keep things fresh and interesting. We will discuss the key lifestyle choices that we made and the practical steps we implemented to sustain our debt-free goal. We will supply hard numbers and examples of how we made our frugal and minimalist lifestyle possible and rewarding. We will provide the critical attributes of a debt slayer, which is the backbone to maintaining the course of becoming debt free. Also, we will offer you tips on how to make additional income to pay off your debt, based on our experience. Lastly, we will provide *The Debt Slayer* checklist that provides a detailed action plan for becoming debt free.

...

This book will also shed light on why being debt free is an attractive financial trait. What's the big deal anyway if debt allows you to live a charming life like everybody else? Ask that question to the student who recently graduated with $37,172 worth of student loan debt but has yet to master Microsoft Excel or any other useful skills, like coding, that the current labor market demands.

They are probably sweating, just like we were, as new graduates from the pressures of massive debt. Unfortunately, this scenario is common, and there is a term for it, it's called the "skills gap". Oh, and that random $37,172 used in the example was not so randomly chosen. That's the average student loan debt for college graduates. Student loan debt is currently a $1.6 trillion crisis according to Forbes. If the student loan crisis is not a wake-up call, then how about the $1 trillion credit card balance for Americans? Still not scary enough? A striking eight out of every 10 Americans carry some type of debt, as mentioned in a CNBC study. Despite the existing culture of borrowing in America that has increased the debt burden, you have the power to obtain financial independence through lifestyle change. It starts with becoming a debt slayer, aggressively getting rid of and avoiding debt.

Countless studies correlate debt to high levels of stress, depression, and anxiety. Who wants to willingly live this way? Not us. Here comes the shocker for the singles. Seventy-five percent of surveyed adults viewed debt as baggage when dating, according to a study conducted by IonTuition. Twelve percent of that sample went as far as ranking debt to be higher baggage than dating someone who has been previously divorced or had children prior to the relationship. Married folks, you are not left off the hook. Currently, one out of every eight divorces are caused by student loan debt, referenced by *USA Today*. Debt in households is increasing year over year and it is adversely changing our lives.

Aside from the emotional trauma and unattractiveness caused by debt, mathematically it does not make sense. The average American will spend close to a whopping $280,000 in interest on debt over their lifetime mentioned by *Money*. Assuming you avoided just 10% of the $280,000 and placed the $28,000 into an index fund for 30 years that provided an 8% average annual rate of return, you would have made $281,754.70 in investment interest versus $280,000 in owed interest. The math is simple. The less you pay in liability interest, the more income that is freed up for assets. The more assets you obtain, the more financial freedom you have. With financial freedom, you can pursue your passions, make career decisions based upon your true desires versus chasing a salary, have greater confidence, travel the world, retire early, and whatever else is desired under the sun.

We believe that financial freedom is the key to living a more fulfilling life. When the dependence of earning money for day-to-day survival is removed, you can simply focus on the things and people that truly matter in your life. Spending time on the initiatives and with people we care about brings forth optimum fulfillment. Harvard Study of Adult Development conducted a study that spanned 75 years and confirms that people with meaningful relationships with family and friends have the most fulfillment in life. In addition, these people lived longer than individuals who did not have strong connections to community. We can attest that during the period of paying off our crazy debt that spiraled out of control took us away from spending time with the people we cared about. Ultimately, we are on the road to achieving financial freedom, and it starts with being debt free. Our goal is to bring everybody with us if you are not already there!

Now, we understand there will be situations where taking out debt is your only option like for college, a mortgage, or starting a business. However, consciously avoiding debt will eliminate frivolous borrowing and save you thousands to hundreds of thousands of dollars. Paying off the debt as fast as possible or completely preventing the debt will increase your available income to put into assets that grow in interest, not charge you interest. Whether you have $37K in student loans or a piece of America's $1 trillion credit card balance, the interest is eating away your disposable income that would have otherwise been available to save, invest, and build financial independence. The sooner you realize that getting out of debt provides a solid financial future and a more fulfilling life, the faster you will adopt a lifestyle of frugality and minimalism to make the loans disappear.

Our goal is to encourage a debt-free lifestyle to help others reach their true potential through financial freedom. We are not financial experts. However, one thing we learned throughout our journey is that having debt ties you down to a lifestyle of focusing on paying debt collectors, distracting you from your passions and gifts. We have always wanted to pursue the opportunity to motivate others to a life of financial freedom, including writing this book. This would not be possible if we were still consumed with side jobs to pay off student loans. When you are not bound by debt, you simply have more financial resources, time, and energy to throw at purpose and people, leading to your best life.

...

This book is dedicated to the millennials who have been plagued by the $1.6 trillion student loan crisis. This book is dedicated to the college students and recent graduates who just cannot get ahead and save that emergency fund cushion before the debt snowball. This book is for the doctors who made headlines for not being able to afford to repay their loans, as well. This book is for your family, our family, and future family members so that they never have to go down the same road as we did. This book is for anyone with debt. This book is for our debt slayers who have been through our journey and paid off all their debt. The journey to financial independence has just begun, as it is often too easy to go back into debt. Lastly, this book is even for the fortunate who have managed to avoid debt altogether. Kudos to all of you and we hope to inspire you to keep this good practice going. We hope to encourage each and every one of you. We hope that you are able to use our story and tips to become debt free and obtain financial freedom. The life you deserve.

PART 1: OUR STORY OF BECOMING DEBT SLAYERS

Chapter 1:

THE HONEYMOON IS OVER

- Tim -

The year of 2014 was the most bittersweet time of our lives, and I remember it like it was yesterday. It seems like we had just finished celebrating LeAnn's graduation from dental school when I successfully defended my graduate research paper to complete my Master's in Economics. I packed my bags the very next day and hopped on a flight from Chicago to Atlanta to join LeAnn for good. Two weeks later, we would unite with friends and family as we said "I do" with the dream of living happily ever after. As newlyweds and recent graduates, we were ready to conquer the world. Now that's just a beautiful story. At least it was until our week-long honeymoon in Costa Rica came to an end and we woke up and smelled the coffee. We were in MAJOR DEBT. Not $5,000, not $20,000, not $70,000 but hundreds of thousands of dollars in debt that would eventually grow to over $429K. It did not take us very long to discover that all our academic achievements, cars, honeymoon, and other significant transactions came with an ugly price. To put the icing on the cake, I was unemployed after interviewing with numerous companies for months. LeAnn was holding our family together with two, part-time dental jobs, and it was evident that there was a financial deficit. We had close to $385K in debt at the time and a SERIOUS income problem.

Throughout the four months of being unemployed, I often felt depressed, frustrated, and emasculated. We were drowning in a sea of debt and I could not do anything about it. Day by day, night by night, interest on the loans grew. I can remember blaming the labor market, rising tuition costs, skills gap, income inequality, and any other social issues prominent in America for the financial mess we had created. We had collectively taken out student loans the size of a mortgage when we had virtually no income. Although the loans were for education, the cost did not seem appropriate. The cost of attending a four-year college and graduate school had drastically changed since our parent's days and we were riding the wave of what would become the trillion-dollar student loan crisis. Sadly, we learned this the hard way. It was time to pay and the honeymoon was clearly over.

Think about it: When did you first realize there was a load of debt weighing you down? How is debt affecting your life?

Chapter 2:

THE MIDDLE-CLASS SQUEEZE

Many may ask, "How does a couple find themselves in over $350K of debt and growing?" Here is the story of how it happened.

- LeAnn -

This story goes back to 2005, when I was a rising senior in high school. Tim and I ironically met that year through a mutual friend. (Yes, we are high school sweethearts!) As my family and I prepared myself for college, anxiety began to rise from the thought of taking out student loans to cover tuition. Despite being very active in high school, involved in various clubs, sports, and community service initiatives, while maintaining over a 4.0 GPA, this was surprisingly not enough to land a full-ride scholarship to any of the schools applied for. Each of the colleges and universities that accepted me only provided partial scholarships - in other words, not enough. Although I was delighted to be accepted into multiple schools, I technically did not have the money to attend any of them.

My family was a typical upper middle-class family. Both parents were college educated and worked in professions that allowed a comfortable lifestyle for me and my sister growing up. I could always count on a memorable Christmas, well-thought-out birthday parties, and fun family vacations. My parents were certainly hard workers. Unfortunately, this was not enough to pay for the college education we would eventually embark on.

Especially not the private school (non-profit) education that is on average 50% higher than in-state public school tuition and room and board. In reflection, my family was experiencing the socioeconomic sweet spot between not being able to afford private college education and not qualifying for additional financial aid due to "too high" of a household income. When middle-class families rack up more student debt than peers from both lower and higher socioeconomic classes, it's referred to as a form of the "Middle-Class squeeze". Little did I know, the full extent of the "middle-class squeeze," was around the corner for me.

Honestly, I could have chosen an in-state public school to increase my chances of obtaining a full-ride scholarship. However, this was not my dream. I was strategic about the schools selected and wanted to attend the college or university that I believed would mold me into the woman I aspired to become. At the same rate, I continued to grow sick by the high opportunity cost associated with the decision of choosing a private college/university over a public one. I was infuriated that such debt burdens were presented to high school students as normal.

As you can see, the stress from student loans burdened my mind prior to even actually acquiring them. Thankfully, my sweet mother searched tirelessly for scholarships. She made sure I worked around the clock on essays for scholarship applications leading up to college. Together, we submitted hundreds of scholarship applications. I was very grateful to receive multiple scholarships for various amounts, $100 here and $1,500 there, etc. My parents also contributed as much as logically and feasibly possible for them. But this combined effort was still not enough to cover the tuition at the private schools. Not even close.

Ultimately, my parents found themselves cosigning with Sallie Mae to help fund my undergraduate education. My parents cosigning for my loans is another issue within itself. Thank God I was able to finish undergrad and graduate school, get a job and be determined to pay off my loans. However, what about the estimated two million students a year who do not complete college after starting a full-time program or the others who find it very difficult to pay off their student loans? It defaults back to their likely middle-age/retirement-aged parents who now technically have the responsibility of paying the bill. There is a student loan crisis.

Throughout my early college years, I often complained about the burden of my student loans. I believe it was completely unfair that a student could work so hard in high school to maintain excellent academics and then be stuck in the middle-class bubble that seemed to be excluded from many income-based scholarships. My search for scholarships did not end as I continued applying for various scholarships throughout my college career. The financial aid staff knew me by name because I stayed in their offices. I even applied for a scholarship that waived the cafeteria fee at school. In my mind, anything helped. By the grace of God, I was finally awarded a scholarship that covered tuition for my junior and senior years. My parents continued to support all my other finances and I finally felt some relief.

In May of 2010, I walked across the stage to accept my diploma and acknowledgment of $40K in student loan debt. Now, I do not regret my undergraduate experience at all, and I am very thankful for the mentorship, sisterhood, growth, and development in my life during that time. However, my positive college experience does not negate the burden I felt from student loans.

As I approached my senior year in college, I started thinking about alternative routes to pay for graduate school. In the dental and medical world, scholarships are not exactly easy to come by. While doing my research, I found that committing to the military or the National

Health Service Corps were the best routes available to fully fund my dental school education. After really praying and meditating about my life, I decided that those options were not for me at that time. In addition, I was feeling defeated and the idea of student loan debt was beginning to feel more and more like a normalcy for me. I had already racked up $40K, why not pile on more? Can I really put a price on my education? Aren't student loans and debt the way of advancement in life leading to success? Before I knew it, I found myself super excited about getting into dental school and following the instructions to fill out financial aid and borrow approximately $45K/year for four years to cover my tuition and room and board throughout the duration of dental school.

Year after year for those four years, I filled out the Free Application for Federal Student Aid (FAFSA). Such irony, it was so amazingly easy and free to apply for debt! After a while I became immune to the effects of what was really going on. I was going through school with my eye on the degree at the end of the tunnel. Eight years prior to my dental school graduation, I was devastated about getting into debt for college, but here I was adding $175K more to the pile of debt. By this point, I was completely settled into the fact that I would be paying my loans back on a 10-year repayment plan once I graduated from dental school.

In May of 2014, I graduated from dental school and proudly accepted my Doctor of Dental Medicine degree. It was a big year in my life because Tim and I were getting married in December of 2014. Life was good until reality hit. One of my gifts was bringing $200K of student loan debt to our marriage.

Think about it: How did you rack up your debt over
time? Prior to getting into debt, did you ever think of
debt as negative or debilitating?

Chapter 3:

INSTANT GRATIFICATION

- Tim -

I like to think the endless snowball of my debt accumulation began when I received my first credit card at the impressionable age of 17. Although the credit limit was only $500, I felt like a real adult by having this shiny piece of plastic in my wallet. That $500 credit limit would somehow flip into a $500 balance on the card. By the time I was a working professional, there were a whopping five credit cards in my wallet with a total balance of over $5,000. That was more than 10 times the amount I started with in high school. The entire time the balances were growing from the spending here and there from my senior year of high school to graduate school, I kept telling myself things like… "I am a responsible guy. I have a job to pay this entire balance off if I wanted to. This MacBook is a *need*, not a want. I'm making over the minimum payments. I have this credit card situation under control." These weekly and sometimes daily conversations with myself were absolutely wrong and continually caused me to go deeper into debt.

I would swipe the credit card to purchase the smaller day-to-day transactions. This behavior was killing my finances—death by a thousand cuts. Eat out after work, swipe. Dinner and a movie date with LeAnn, swipe. Gas to get to work, swipe. The list continues. I would eventually pay down the balance, I thought to myself, but not right away. And definitely not down to zero. I thought I would magically get a bonus or increase in pay to clean up the gradually increasing credit card bills. Never happened. The logic behind how I used my credit cards back in the day is still beyond me. The only explanation that I can pull out of the hat is that I was attempting to live a luxurious lifestyle on a poor man's budget. Or maybe my credit cards were mismanaged for instant gratification. I remember a time when I signed up for a new credit card to purchase a new MacBook for creative projects. In reflection, it was clear that instant gratification was getting out of control at that point. I had never swiped the shiny plastic for a large transaction until this purchase.

Despite my tendency to mismanage credit cards for the sake of instant gratification, I have always been practical with money in other areas. For example, I maintained a savings account for financial independence and major purchases since childhood. In middle school, I would save the lunch money my parents gave me daily to build a fund for my outings to the movies and candy splurges. Once I got my first job in high school working at a video store, where I ultimately met LeAnn through a coworker, I bought my first car in cash. It was a fixer upper for sure that lasted maybe a few months before I eventually sold it to someone else due to the overwhelming mechanical work it required. However, I valued the principle of paying cash for major purchases - even if it was a piece of trash, in this case. In 2009, after saving money since my video store job in high school, I purchased my second car, a shiny inferno-red 2006 Chrysler Sebring for $6,000 in cash. A few years later, I would purchase a motorcycle for another couple of thousand dollars with cash, saved from working my first job out of college.

While buying vehicles with cash was a no-brainer, paying cash for college never registered to me. My parents were big on education, being educators and pastors themselves, so going to college was inevitable. Growing up around the college my father taught mathematics at allowed me to determine that this was the school I would attend early on, which was great. However, I never really thought about how I would pay for college. This question never crossed my mind primarily for two reasons. By 2006, it was the norm to take out student loans for college. Secondly, my parents knew that if my father continued to work at the private college through my matriculation there, my tuition cost would be completely waived. That's exactly what my father did to pay for not only my four-year college tuition but my older brother's as well. This was a tuition waiver offered to full-time faculty members and their dependent children established to help strengthen the college's human resources through continued education and this added benefit.

Yes, I know you are trying to figure out how I accumulated such massive debt when my undergraduate degree was nearly costless. Well, not entirely. Since I knew my tuition would be waived going into college, I submitted virtually zero applications for scholarships- the total opposite of LeAnn's experience of aimlessly submitting hundreds of scholarship applications to make ends meet for tuition. Shortly after enrolling in school my freshman year, I realized that room and board was not covered by the faculty tuition waiver. That was an automatic $10,000 to sleep in a cold dorm room on campus and eat my favorite food, pizza, every day in the cafeteria. Living on campus was actually a mandate for all first-year students, so I had no choice but to take out student loans for this part. Unfortunately, I did not actively try to secure scholarships until finding out about this expense a few weeks before my freshman year began.

It amazes me that I could have technically been paid to go to college if I secured enough scholarships on top of my tuition waiver. While I did eventually obtain multiple scholarships, including the Hope Scholarship, a statewide scholarship for students who maintained a 3.0 GPA or higher attending public colleges/universities in the state of Georgia, they were insignificant amounts. For instance, the Hope Scholarship only awarded me a little over $2K per academic year due to the private school limitation. In addition, I picked up a few more scholarships throughout my undergraduate matriculation, but still found myself in over $20,000 in student loan debt by the time I walked across the stage in 2010 to receive my bachelor's degree. Living expenses from being an undergrad college student added up with minor income streams here and there. When it came time to embark on graduate school two years later, I had been convinced that student loans were the only way to get a master's degree. Besides, student loans were "good debt." At least that was the consensus for the masses at the time, which I sadly believed. Once again, I would attend another private university, except there was no tuition waiver or corporate tuition reimbursement program. To make the financial burden worse, I chose an out-of-state school in a high-cost-of-living city, known as Chicago. I will admit that I thoroughly enjoyed perusing this city, meeting some really good people, and my master's program overall. However, I enjoyed it a little too much. I got an apartment overlooking Lake Michigan in a premier downtown location in close proximity to my school, which was one of the most expensive neighborhoods in the city. The average one-bedroom apartment goes for $1,660 in Chicago, which is currently the 10th-most expensive rental market in the U.S. I paid $900 a month to share a two-bedroom apartment with another student. Since my graduate program was for two years, I would spend an estimated $21,600 on housing alone.

OK, here is the part where your stomach can start to get uneasy like mine did from the enormous debt load. My graduate program was about $25,000 per academic year and I would net out with over $50,000 on tuition alone. If you add in living expenses, like groceries from Trader Joe's, eating out at Chipotle, hanging out with friends at Wrigleyville, traveling between Chicago and Atlanta to see LeAnn, and other expenses, we get another $10K-$15K over two years. I was easily approaching a monstrous $100,000 in debt from graduate school alone. My logic behind taking out the loans was that I could pay it back with one or two years' worth of future salary. This reasoning was flawed. It did not even consider basic expenses like housing and groceries, let alone a wedding or the fact that I would be unemployed for a few months shortly after my graduation. It was a made-up forecast in my head to keep me comfortable with the adverse debt burden I was accumulating.

Although I started graduate school with savings, this was quickly depleted living in a high-cost-of-living city. I resorted to student loans the entire two years in Chicago. I fell into this trap chasing instant gratification and a luxurious lifestyle I could not afford, leveraging student debt and credit cards. I now had approximately $122,830.88 in student loan debt combined from undergrad and graduate school.

Think about it: Is your story similar, falling into the instant gratification lifestyle?

Chapter 4:

ENOUGH IS ENOUGH

Here we were in December of 2014, with four degrees, recently married and in $355K of debt. The dust was finally settling, and it was not pretty.

- Tim -

LeAnn and I were trying to establish our new life together and the anxiety was building. The student life was over and after carelessly borrowing money throughout undergrad and graduate school, it was time to pay. There were many occasions I would wake up in the middle of the night with a pounding heart from the pressure of the loans that were growing in interest by the day. I was in a unique situation where I was overqualified for entry-level positions but had minimum experience for mid-level positions. Companies entertained me but wanted to see solid work experience, which I lacked like any other recent graduate. The endless cycle of applying, interviewing, and receiving no offer ruined me inside.

Meanwhile, LeAnn was supporting our household as a newly-graduated dentist. Although she was able to command a competitive wage as a dentist in the marketplace, having one income was not sustainable for our debt burden. We had an estimated $350K in student loan debt alone with interest growing close to $1,000 each month. Before our marriage, LeAnn had always planned to rapidly pay off all her student loans once she graduated. Adding my $100K+ in debt was not a part of the equation. However, she was forced to abandon making significant loan payments just to keep the household afloat. This was a major setback for her as she absolutely hated debt. As you can imagine, strong tension grew in our home from the financial mess both of us had accumulated over the years. This was not a healthy situation for a young, newly-married couple. We had to make a change. Although blaming our current job situations and colleges for taking the money we did not have seemed appropriate, the debt problem at hand stemmed from the decisions we made.

- LeAnn -

Marriage was not starting out quite like I imagined but I was ready to take on the challenges of being the sole provider in the house for a couple of months. I knew Tim would find the right opportunity for him soon. Little did I know, every day would be an emotional roller coaster. As confident as I was in supporting Tim, I never considered the emotional toll that this situation was taking on him and soon me. Being a married man and not able to provide for your family was an extremely big deal for him. As a young new wife, I did not know how to truly handle this situation. I started out doing everything a supportive wife should do. I made an active effort to be very encouraging and understanding, while showing my willingness and readiness to provide for our new little family. As time passed, I was slowly becoming mentally and physically drained from the negative energy in the house. There was only so much encouraging I could do before I needed encouragement myself. The supportive wife turned into the frustrated wife at our finances. I did not understand why Tim could not have a three-course meal prepared for us when I got home from work since he was at home all day. I felt like I was working hard and Tim was having a grand time relaxing at home. In reality, this was not the case. He was busy throughout the day, endlessly applying and searching for opportunities. Eventually, I started claiming "my money" when referencing our finances. The union I was so excited about just a couple of months prior, turned into a clear divide when it came to our finances. We were both feeling defeated and seeking a change.

Finally, we got a break when Tim landed a job in business analytics. We were both employed now but for some reason it still felt like we were stagnant with our finances. I was confused at the phenomenon of how two educated individuals with professional careers could still be living paycheck to paycheck. By paycheck to paycheck, I do not mean we were struggling to pay the bills, but I do mean we did not have a lot of wiggle room with our finances or very much money left over for savings and investments. When I evaluated our expenses, the largest sum of money was going toward debt repayment. Basically, we took out loans to go to school, so we could work and spend our paychecks on repaying the loans. This is not the financial future I imagined for myself. At this rate, I felt like I should have opted not to go to graduate school and take on the burden of student loans. Even if my income was less, without the debt, I could have been increasing my net worth and on a faster track to financial freedom. Marriage brought another aspect to the equation.

Tim had his own bag of student loans and consumer debt. We had weekly and sometimes daily discussions about debt destroying our financial future. The amount of money that flew out of the door toward loan payments was infuriating and insane. The only solution was to commit to paying as much money as possible toward the loans so we could get rid of them as soon as possible. The faster we paid off the debt, the faster we were on our way to building our net worth, creating a legacy for our family, and cultivating freedom. In essence, the faster we could live the lifestyle we envisioned for our family. Thankfully, since we had already stepped into a financial fire in our marriage right out of the gate, it did not take much for Tim to get on board with paying off all the debt as soon as possible.

Think about it: When did you decide that enough is enough? Have you ever reached a point where your loans and debt were emotionally and mentally draining? Have you buried your debt in the back of your mind to avoid facing it?

Chapter 5:

TAKING ACTION

March 2015

- Tim -

Now we had dual income for our dual loans. The journey was not over though, it was just beginning. We had enough cash flow to pay down debt in addition to covering the bills, but the debt was still not disappearing. Since LeAnn had always fiercely hated debt and had managed to live without it until student loans, paying on them for the standard 10-year term was non-negotiable. After experiencing trauma, depression, and a diminished feeling of manliness from being crushed by debt during unemployment, I knew that becoming debt free was the only way to take back control of my life. It was like we were mice in a wheel, spinning, spinning, and spinning. The "rat race" concept became more apparent than ever before.

The first thing we did was create a list of all our debt from student loans to consumer loans. We had to know exactly what we owed to determine what would set us free. Then we began researching ways to get out of debt. Shortly after doing our research, we decided that the debt snowball was the best strategy for us to chip away at the loans. This method required us to list and pay off all our loans from smallest to largest.

The Debt Snowball
The debt snowball is a debt payment strategy where you pay off debt from smallest to largest, regardless of the associated interest rate. This method was popularized by Dave Ramsey and uses the psychology of quick wins as a reinforcer to keep you motivated on the journey. This is the method we used to get out of debt.

It was at this moment that we began to take ownership of our financial mistakes. What I mean by this is that we owned every single financial obligation, mistake, and blemish life threw at us over the years by listing it on the debt snowball to ultimately pay.

That list of close to 40 debts was honestly the most depressing Excel spreadsheet ever seen but also the most liberating!

Loan Type	Original Balance
Student Loan	$39,548.86
Student Loan	$36,602.25
Student Loan	$35,331.16
Student Loan	$33,197.66
Student Loan	$27,318.05
Student Loan	$20,500.00
Student Loan	$20,500.00
Auto Loan	$20,350.80
Student Loan	$18,237.36
Student Loan	$17,549.69
Student Loan	$15,000.00

Chart Continued

Loan Type	Original Balance
Student Loan	$15,000.00
Student Loan	$10,571.19
Student Loan	$8,290.87
Student Loan	$8,290.87
Student Loan	$7,877.00
Student Loan	$7,685.36
Student Loan	$6,833.00
Student Loan	$5,000.00
Student Loan	$4,894.17
Student Loan	$2,000.00
Student Loan	$2,000.00
Credit Card	$1,994.47
Credit Card	$1,244.28
Credit Card	$996.25
Collections	$986.00
Credit Card	$721.19
Tax Bill	$587.00
IOU	$500.00
Credit Card	$498.00
Medical Bill	$405.88
Medical Bill	$223.58
Total	**$370,734.94**

There were old medical bills, credit card balances, student loans of course, and even an old $500 loan I borrowed from LeAnn way back in college. OK, we probably could have left that last item off, but I was serious about taking ownership over our financial future. In March of 2015, we purchased a crossover SUV that added another $20K to the debt snowball above. We probably could have found a cheaper vehicle to replace LeAnn's 10-year old Honda Civic that was deemed totaled from a fender bender, but we were set on having new and nice. This purchase that did not reflect the frugal lifestyle we needed to follow more closely to slay our debt. We now had a total debt of $370,734.94.

Think about it: Where are you on your debt free journey? Are your daily decisions aligned with your financial goals?

Chapter 6:

WHAT HAPPENED TO OUR TESLA?

December 2015

- LeAnn -

By the end of 2015, approaching the beginning of year two of our debt-free journey and marriage, we were making a little headway on the debt. However, after evaluating the hard numbers, our total family debt had only decreased by 5%.

That financial gain was almost completely voided when we purchased a second vehicle for Tim in November of 2015. He previously sold his shiny red Sebring in 2012 to embrace public transportation while attending graduate school in Chicago. Upon returning to Atlanta at the end of 2014, he never purchased a new car. His parents were kind enough to lend him one of their vehicles periodically, while we carpooled to and from work for close to a year in the crossover SUV we purchased earlier that year in March. Sharing a vehicle allowed us to save money by avoiding this major purchase as long as we could and throw more money at our debt. After holding out as long as practically possible, we bought a used 2013 Nissan Leaf and added another $14,680.75 auto loan to the debt snowball in December of 2015.

March 2015 Debt	$370,734.94
December 2015 Debt	$352,600.76
Debt Reduction	$18,134.18
Auto Loan + $14,680.75	
Final December 2015 Debt	$367,281.51

- Tim -

Purchasing the Leaf was one of the hardest decisions I personally made on our debt-free journey. I have always been a big fan of luxury cars and had plans to purchase the Tesla Model 3, a state-of-the-art fully electric sedan that was a future release. Elon Musk, the founder and CEO of Tesla Motors, was a role model of mine at the time and there was nothing wrong you could say about him or the cars. I was a fan to say the least. In my Business Strategy course in graduate school, I even co-authored a 21-page research paper analyzing Tesla's market position and business strategy. This was obviously a deep and highly-premeditated purchase. Buying a Tesla was not a question.

However, the four months of being unemployed and not being able to provide for my family left a lasting impression on me. My future buying behavior would change for the better, forever. Avoiding that pain of struggling financially far outweighed buying a luxury vehicle that would provide temporary pleasure. LeAnn made many financial sacrifices for our family just a few months prior and I was more committed to our future and legacy than ever before. So I did the rational thing by opting for a vehicle option that was 64% cheaper. Looking back on it, this decision saved us an estimated $27K on our future debt snowball.

NISSAN LEAF VS. TESLA MODEL 3	
Vehicle	**Price**
Tesla Model 3	$41,860
Nissan Leaf	$14,680
Savings	$27,180

Regardless, we purchased one new vehicle and one used vehicle which added two auto loans in 2015, pushing out our timeline to debt freedom. This was not the behavior of a couple who was trying to become debt free like yesterday. We needed to make more drastic changes in our lifestyle choices. At this rate, it would take us over a decade to reach debt freedom.

Think About It: What sacrifices are you willing to make to achieve your debt free goal? Is it driving an old car? Living with your parents? Missing out on international vacations with friends?

Chapter 7:

CONSOLIDATING OUR DEBT

- LeAnn -

With the end goal in mind of cultivating a lifestyle of freedom and legacy, we had to go back to the drawing board. Our next game plan was looking into debt consolidation. After doing our research, Tim and I both decided to consolidate our student loans to obtain lower interest rates while organizing all our individual loans under one servicer, individually. I researched various companies and options for loan consolidation. Ultimately, I chose the company that would result in the lowest interest rate and did not have any penalties for paying the loans off early. The American Dental Association (ADA) had a contract with Mohela, a federal student loan management company, that allowed members to save .25% and an additional .25% for enrolling in automatic draft for monthly payments above the offered rate. This was the best offer for me and allowed my interest rate to drop from a varying 5.25% to 4.5%. When consolidating, I also selected a seven-year repayment to term to put the pressure on myself a little more than the standard 10-year repayment plan.

Tim chose MyFedLoan Servicing to consolidate all his loans under one roof. Coincidentally, MyFedLoan Servicing is the same company I switched from when I consolidated. Consolidation really comes down to whatever company gives you the best interest rate and allows you to pay off your loans early without penalty. He had a handful of private, Stafford, and Plus loans from undergrad and graduate school and MyFedLoan made it extremely easy to make one simple payment. He also received a .25% reduction in interest paid on loans by setting up an auto draft for monthly payment. Tim later explored refinancing again with SoFi to get the interest rate on his student loans even lower. They offered him a slightly lower interest rate that would have saved us only $2,000 over a 10-year repayment period. With the intention to pay the loans much sooner than 10 years, we decided to pass on the offer.

STUDENT LOAN CONSOLIDATION

Student loan consolidation allowed us to reduce the interest paid on all of our student loans by .25 - .5%. HIGHLY recommend.

We knew it would take more than debt consolidation to conquer our goals. Therefore, we were actively seeking any opportunities to make as much money as possible during this period. I was blessed to be offered a role as the lead dentist in a different office which came with additional responsibilities but opportunity for increased income. Tim switched from a job in the public sector to the private sector to bring home more income. These career advancements played vital roles in the debt reduction.

Think About It: Would student loan consolidation be beneficial in your situation?

Chapter 8:

BECOMING DEBT SLAYERS

December 2016

Another year passed and it was December 2016. We continued snowballing the debt, paying the minimum on all the loans and extra toward the smallest loan to pay it off the fastest. Then, moving on to the next smallest loan. We were finally picking up some momentum. By the end of our second year on the journey, our total debt had decreased by close to 18% to $302K. This was over three times the debt reduction of 5% obtained in our first year.

December 2015 Debt	$367,281.51
December 2016 Debt	$302,183.97
Debt Reduction	**$65,097.54**

However, we began to lose motivation and drive around this same period. It had been 24 months into our debt snowball, the process required lots of sacrifices and our gas was running low, like any normal human at that point. What was going on here? We truly felt like we were going above and beyond to achieve debt cancelation, but still had another $300K to go after two years!

We knew that if there was a fighting chance to become debt free, it had to be done quickly. There was no way we could stomach living this intensely for another estimated five years (timeline based on paying off $65K the previous year). We determined that the remaining of our path to debt freedom could no longer be a comfy stroll of just actively paying off debt and being more frugal with our money. We needed to be extremely aggressive with debt cancelation. Instead of paying debt, we had to "slay" our debt! It was no longer a game. The debt we had accumulated over the years was standing in the way of our freedom, purpose, and family legacy. It was time to get mad and combative with our debt once and for all.

The time had come for us to sit down and truly evaluate the finances in our household. Honestly, we were not living a frugal lifestyle entirely. It's safe to say we were living a "frugal when we want to be" lifestyle. After looking in the mirror, we had traveled to some of the most amazing countries in the world, purchased a new SUV, and spent money on lots of other luxurious things. There was a lifestyle and financial goal contradiction. Although we managed to get the debt snowball rolling, plus cut household expenses in many areas, we were still trying to live a luxurious lifestyle when we needed a strict frugal lifestyle to become debt slayers. Our luxurious buying behavior was fighting against the financial advances that we were achieving from the debt snowball. Periodically living luxuriously over the past two years ultimately caused a money leakage of $31K that could have been used to eliminate our debt. We overspent on two vehicles, knowing we could have found reliable cars for around $5K and our foreign trips cost us thousands. Sadly, these were just a few obvious transactions but not all. Becoming a debt slayer was a necessity and that is what we did.

Think About It: Consider some of your recent purchases. Could you have made different decisions to produce a better financial outcome? (Remember, you can budget for luxury or nonessential items in the future, just not when you are getting out debt.)

MONEY LEAKAGE FROM LUXURY PURCHASES	
New Crossover SUV (2015)	$15,000
Second Vehicle (2015)	$9,000
International Trip (2015)	$3,000
International Trip (2016)	$3,000
Total Leakage	**$30,000**

March 2017

After reflecting on our shortcomings from poor lifestyle choices and behaviors toward getting out of debt at the halfway mark, we turned to our budget to address and correct the issues from their roots. We immediately committed to a tight budget/consistent frugal lifestyle.

FRUGALITY
Frugality is the act of spending wisely and intentionally with your money. Living this type of lifestyle requires active management of your finances. Frugality is a necessary trait of a debt slayer.

- LeAnn -

Between the two of us, I am the budgetnista. I actually genuinely enjoy creating, following and seeing the fruits of the labor manifest in savings from a budget. However, becoming a debt slayer required a budget that was a little more detailed than those I previously created. I sat down at the end of every month and looked at our expected income for the upcoming month, living expenses, and any additional expenses I could foresee. I combed through every single line item looking for any area possible to reduce the expense, even if just by $5. But the work does not stop there. I continually updated our budget throughout the month, tracking our expenses and ensuring we were still on target. Not to mention, I had to make sure Tim was staying on track as well! Just kidding, he was pretty good at staying within the budget. After all, we had debt to slay! Weekly check-ins were necessary to make sure we were on target for the month and had as much left over as possible to throw at the debt.

BUDGETING

Using your actual or estimated income and predicted expenses to consciously track your financial trajectory for a period of time. Being a debt slayer requires following a very strict budget.

In an attempt to be as aggressive as possible, we had shockingly low dollar amounts for line items in our budget. For instance, our restaurant budget was $25 per month, our pocket money was $50 apiece per month and we even allocated $0 for a few other common line items in most budgets. (More on this in the Budgeting/Frugality chapter.) Here is a little snapshot of a few line items.

Groceries	**$300**
Pocket Money (each)	**$50**
Miscellaneous	**$50**
Restaurant	**$25**
Clothes Shopping	**$0**
Entertainment	**$0**

We eventually found Dave Ramsey and the Baby Steps program, which led to us using his web-based EveryDollar budgeting app. Prior, I was doing our budget by pen and paper, the old fashion way. This tool was helpful because it gave 24/7 visibility to the both of us and streamlined the budgeting process by carrying over your line items from the previous month. In addition, his 7-step program helped us trim the fat in our household. We took down our emergency savings to only $1,000 and paid the difference toward our loans. This was Baby Step 1 of 7. We were undoubtedly frightened by the idea of living essentially paycheck to paycheck without a larger savings cushion. However, mentally, we were debt slayers at this point and would conquer the debt at all costs.

Next, we cashed out all our **non-retirement** investments, and paid our debt with the proceeds. (Emphasis on non-retirement because we did not touch any established retirement accounts such as 401(k)s.) This was another financial decision not for the faint-hearted. Yes, we understood that there was an opportunity cost of giving up interest that could have been made on our investments that were sold to pay debt.

However, the interest we were being charged from our large student loan balance far outpaced any interest that was being generated from mutual funds. More importantly, we made strides with paying down debt by this decision. Our debt decreased by a breathtaking $104,293.41 from December of 2016 to June of 2017.

December 2016 Debt	$302,183.97
June 2017 Debt	$197,890.56
Debt Reduction	$104,293.41

Honestly, not having a healthy emergency fund savings and any non-retirement investment accounts made us more ambitious because losing was not an option. If we had both lost our jobs, we would have been on the streets. We had no immediate cash reserves and would have only had $1,000 on hand to cover maybe 60% of our bills for the following month. As a result, the inverse of homelessness happened. We grinded like no one else on our jobs and received promotions, raises, and were actually rewarded from the hunger to be debt free. As our incomes increased, we remained consistent with paying everything minus monthly expenses and our tithes to the debt that remained. We did not want to relive the moments at the beginning of our marriage when our financial future felt like a black hole. Nor the time when we did not have a concrete plan for debt repayment and we were both stressed and infuriated with our loans. Keeping our goal in mind: cultivate freedom and legacy, we pressed on.

- Tim -

Throughout year three, we were hacking away at the loans like two debt slayers. Things were going exceptionally well for us until the trimming of the fat began to reach the bones. About 50% of our loans were paid off, but we needed to make some tough decisions to close out the debt while adversity and life changes kept hitting us along the way. For example, I had to close down shop on the mobile app company I formed with a business partner during graduate school. As an entrepreneur at heart, this was extremely difficult. I had put blood, sweat, tears, and of course thousands of dollars into this venture over the past few years. However, it was sucking up cash and energy I could no longer provide due to my debt obligations. So my partner and I agreed to dissolve the business and part ways. This was a huge pain point for me along the journey. I had experienced firsthand how debt could rip away dreams overnight. As much as I would like to blame the decision solely on cash flow, in reality, my creativity had stifled, ambition had decreased, and the stress from wearing too many hats while getting out of debt was unbearable. This was an awakening of how debt was ripping away the intangibles I valued in my life.

. . .

A few months later, we got a visit from the tax man, also known as the IRS. I might add that this was not a friendly drop by. With only a few more student loans remaining, we received the largest tax bill I had ever seen. The job promotions we received throughout the year caused our household to enter into a new tax bracket that we did not appropriately account for in paycheck deductions. It was time to pay an estimated $10,000.

Shortly after, we met with our financial advisor, Helen, to seek help on avoiding tax surprises like this in the future. She recommended withholding more income from our checks for the remaining 2018 to ensure we did not owe as much next year. Also, she pointed out that since we had decreased our contributions to our 401(k)'s during the year of 2017 to pay off more debt, our taxable income increased. The increase in income plus low contributions to our tax-deferred retirement accounts were a recipe for a $10K tax bill. We made the recommended adjustments and kept chugging along. However, this was a major setback to our debt snowball plan, and it was crippling mentally to watch all that money go out the window.

$10,000 Tax Bill
to our debt snowball

We had to pick up speed somewhere to keep our sanity, so we relied on minimalism. We began selling everything of value in our house that did not add value to our lives, for additional income. We actively questioned random items in our apartment to determine if it made us feel good, caused stress, or neither. If it was the latter two and it was worth more than a dollar, the item was sold. Clothes, shoes, books, hair styling equipment, and anything that did not add value to our lives were all sold. I religiously posted these items on eBay and Amazon, and some were sold to retailers who bought and sold gently used clothes and technology.

MINIMALISM

The lifestyle of being conscious of your possessions, requiring constant questioning of the items that do or do not add value to your life. We leveraged a minimalist lifestyle to make additional money and avoid unnecessary spending.

As a natural minimalist, this part of the journey came easy to me. When an item did not bring me joy, I sold it or gifted it, most likely to my younger brother, even if it was valuable. Somehow, I was just born this way. I once gave away a pair of $400 Ferragamo loafers to a college student because I felt like he was deserving of them. I had witnessed this young man's commitment to school and passion for helping others and noticed he wore my size. Note, these $400 shoes were a gift from a mentor of mine who I'm sure would appreciate the gesture himself. It was a no-brainer to give them away.

Eventually, LeAnn got the hang of minimalism after watching the amazing documentary "The Minimalist." This documentary was about two men known as the Minimalists who drastically improved the quality of their life by adopting this lifestyle (check out the documentary). We collectively practiced minimalism daily to see what items we could sell and to avoid any spontaneous shopping desires that may creep up at this part of our journey. We even sold the Leaf to get the last 25% of our debt down. Embracing minimalism by selling a car and other items in our household was still not enough though.

Side Hustles

The only thing left to do that we had not done yet was pick up side jobs for additional income. That is precisely what we did. We leveraged everything from our laptops to our cars as means for ways to generate additional income. Our day jobs require us to be present and fully engaged so we had to get creative when looking for side hustles. Initially, the thought of adding anything else to our schedule seemed impossible. However, where there is a will, there is a way. We were grinding. (More on side hustles in Chapter 13: The 30+ Side Hustles of a Debt Slayer.)

December 2017

- LeAnn -

As the third year of our journey came to an end and the fourth year began, we had reduced the debt by 68%. We were sitting at a balance of $120K down from $370K in March of 2015. The $120K was still a big pill to swallow though. We were by no means feeling relieved and were still deep in debt. Student loans was still a stressful topic in our house, but we had a plan, so we knew the end of this journey was somewhere in sight.

March 2015 Debt	$370,734.94
December 2017 Debt	$120,381.05
Debt Reduction	$250,353.89

In fact, the pressure was on even stronger as we found out we were expecting our first child due in August 2018. We were still living in a one-bedroom apartment with a budget that only allowed for necessities. This was not exactly the environment I dreamed of bringing a baby home to. Decorating a nursery was only a dream in my world. The "nursery" was going to be the 4-foot space between my side of the bed and the door to the bathroom. Putting a changing station in our room left about eight inches between the dresser/changing table and our bed for Tim and me to walk from one side of the room to the other. It sounds a little crazy after revisiting this situation. Thankfully by this time in our journey, my mind was so focused on getting out of debt that moving before the baby was born was never an option. Instead we chose to see our small apartment, that allowed us to meet our budget, as an opportunity to be close to our newborn. Financial freedom was more important than decorating a nursery that our child will not remember.

August 2018

Little did we know, we would continue to run into dilemmas with our housing situation. With high hopes and ambitions, we dreamed of having our debt paid off by the time the baby was born, so we could move into a nice two-bedroom apartment. However, around the time our son, Liam, entered the world, we were still sitting at about $27K of student loan debt.

December 2017 Debt	$120,381.05
August 2018 Debt	$26,992.39
Debt Reduction	**$93,288.66**

Our apartment lease was up in November and we had some tough decisions to make. Thankfully, we live in the same city as our parents and that is always an option. However, staying at our parents' house was not a resource that we ever considered to help us nail the debt. At the tail end of our journey, we were going to move into the two-bedroom apartment and risk paying on the loans an additional month. We were so close that we did not feel like we needed to stay in a one-bedroom but weren't quite ready for the increase in rent that came with a two-bedroom. Eventually we just decided to pull the trigger for the bigger apartment.

One day while at work, I received a phone call from the new leasing office manager. They stated there were construction delays on the new apartment site and we could push back our move-in date or move into a finished unit and then later move into the unit we wanted. Immediately, I thought about the money we could save by staying with my parents. This was a sign from God to not waver on our journey at the very tail end. The issue would be running this past Tim. Staying at my parents' house was probably his biggest nightmare. Not due to my parents but just the dependency he would feel, as a very independent person. His reaction was exactly as I expected, and it was not an easy conversation. However, after weighing the benefits and reviewing our financial goals, we realized that sometimes it takes stepping out of your comfort zone to reach your goals. Meanwhile, my parents were standing at the door with open arms ready and excited for their new house guests, especially their grandson.

HOUSE HACKING
House Hacking is a phrase coined by the real-estate investor, Brandon Turner, taking place when a homeowner rents out their home to renters who ultimately pay their mortgage and some.

For six weeks, we were able to live rent free. This was our final stretch. We are so grateful for my parents, the Ballentines, for allowing us to crash with them as our debt-free journey came to an end. Shortly after Thanksgiving, Tim and I sat in my parents' kitchen and submitted the last payment to his student loans! I was so excited that I did a happy dance across the house while Tim was still taking it in. The feeling of submitting the final payment on student loans still makes my heart skip a beat and brings a smile to my face.

Debt Free: December 3, 2018

On December 3, 2018, our last student loan payment had posted as paid in full. We were debt free! Reality had really sunk in and our hearts were filled with joy. Paying off $429K in four years was more than what I prayed for and ever imagined. We had worked so hard for this moment and the feeling was surreal.

…

Today, we are humbled to say we are debt free. We are still in awe when reflecting on this insane four-year road of throwing all our money, time, and energy at debt. Just the thought of debt gives us anxiety, and we can still feel the crushing effect. We vividly remember the emotional roller coaster we rode at the beginning of our marriage. The depression around unemployment, the supportive days, the frustrated days, the anger when half of the paycheck disappears to loan payments. All of those moments are still so real and raw. However, it was this crazy financial journey that instilled so many key values and attributes in us that would be leveraged for a lifetime. We developed willpower, teamwork, accountability, financial transparency, better communication, and discovered more of our dreams throughout the process of getting out of debt. It feels good to owe no man nothing but to love them.

More importantly, it is incredible to know that our son who was born at the end of our debt-slayer journey, will not inherit debt and will be passed on a legacy of financial freedom. Staying focused on the debt-free goal through the frugal and minimalist lifestyle helped us immensely to weather all the adversity that came our way. Being debt free has allowed us to clear our minds and begin to focus on living a more fulfilling life that is not driven by bills.

Hopefully, our story has been an encouragement to your own personal journey. We are grateful that God has blessed us with this crazy journey of getting out of debt so that we could share it with you. If you are anything like us, your journey to becoming debt free will not be easy. However, with these fundamental lifestyle changes and tips provided, we are confident you can do it!

Think About It: Have you established a budget? Do characteristics such as frugality and minimalism come natural to you? (P.S. More tips to come later in the book on budgeting and frugality! Keep reading! ☺)

THE RECAP

We got married and went on a honeymoon in December 2014. Our combined starting debt was $355,430.04.

Our debt reduction over four years:

Date	Debt Reduction	Debt Balance
Dec. 2014	N/A	$355,430.04
Dec. 2015	($11,851.47)	$367,281.51
Dec. 2016	$65,097.54	$302,183.97
Dec. 2017	$181,802.92	$120,381.05
Dec. 2018	$120,381.05	$0

Changes we made on our debt-free journey that led to paying off debt and becoming debt slayers:

Year	Changes
2015	Debt Snowball
2016	Student Loan Consolidation
BECAME DEBT SLAYERS	
2017	Tight Budget, Reduced Savings to $1K, Cashed out Non-retirement Investments, Job Promotions
2018	Minimalism Lifestyle, Side Hustles, House Hacking

Total Debt Paid Including Interest Over 4-Year Journey

$429,768.17

Current Debt Balance: $0

PART 2: LIVING A MORE FULFILLING LIFE

Chapter 9:

WHY GET OUT OF DEBT?

The four-year journey to paying off six-figure debt was an intense one. We went through every emotional state from depression to joy. There were disagreements, times of celebration, and many moments of just plain hard grind. Many people along the way were fascinated by our tenacity to be debt free but did not understand why we would make so many sacrifices. After all, we were at a time in our lives that some would consider "prime time," late 20s, newly married, and launching professional careers. So why exactly would we sacrifice this time in our life to pay off debt? In essence, we recognized very early in our life, that we wanted a life of freedom and building legacy. We did not want to be bound by debt and bills, we wanted to make decisions that were passion based and not financial based. Essentially, we wanted to live a more fulfilling life.

However, for those who may still be asking why get out of debt, here are a few reasons: debt in America is an epidemic that is negatively impacting the lives of every demographic and generation. Currently, student loans are a $1.6 trillion catastrophe that has led one out of every four student loan borrowers to delinquency. The National Consumer Law Center estimates $125 billion in delinquent debt alone. Imagine how this debt is adversely affecting the finances of the millennials (born between 1980 and 1994) or Generation X (born between 1965-1979) to save, invest, and buy property. What about Generation Z (born between 1995 and 2015) who will also be graduating from college with debt, right about now (in 2020)? Sadly, student loans have reached the baby boomer generation, too. Student loan debt for age 60 and older has quadrupled over the last decade according to the Consumer Financial Protection Bureau. Talk about late retirement. No matter how you slice and dice the data, the average household in the U.S. still has $139,500 in debt referenced by nasdaq.com. In addition, the nation's credit card balance is over $1 trillion, with an average individual credit card balance of $6,375. As a result, it is changing the way we live. Aside from the mess America has collectively accumulated, here are a few good reasons why nobody should ever want debt.

YOUR WHY

Your personal "why" is the driver for your debt-free journey. Knowing why you want to be debt free is as important as being debt free. This discovery is critical to know because it is the very reason to be debt free. This is your reinforcer. Being debt free to be debt free is not good enough. You simply will not make it to the finish line without the purpose and motivation. Fortunately, finding your "why" to conquer the debt is usually apparent. If not, just think about what keeps you up at night. Find your why and spark the motivation!

- LeAnn -

For example, my initial why for being debt free was simply having full autonomy over my income. I worked hard to earn a decent living. Therefore, I did not want to hand it over to someone else unwillingly. The goal was to allocate my check as I saw fit. Having full control over my money gave me peace of mind. With a personal student loan bill of $220K total and monthly payments of $2.5K, I literally felt enslaved to the lender. I was drowning in a sea that was only getting deeper due to interest by the day. I pursued a profession that I thought would allow me to provide a decent lifestyle for myself. However, I quickly realized that paying $2.5K per month for 10 years to a lender was going to obliterate my expected income potential. Also, I became disgusted at the fact that the $220K borrowed would become $300K throughout repayment, due to interest. These numbers did not even include Tim's debt. Coming to terms with throwing this kind of money away was impossible for me. As I matured, got married, and started a family my "why" began to evolve. It became much deeper. I began to center my why around building generational wealth, determining my own retirement, not being confined to a standard career track, and living a life without financial constraints.

- Tim -

One concept that continually reminds me of why debt free is imperative is lifestyle freedom. I desire a lifestyle of flexibility, spontaneity, mobility, and freedom to pursue passions. Maybe even hobbies again. It became apparent during our journey to become debt slayers that having debt would not provide this ideal lifestyle. In fact, the debt I accumulated extended the opposite of lifestyle freedom. The debt chained me to the "rat race." I woke up every morning to work, stress about debt, sleep, and repeat. I was in bondage to lenders and had zero freedom. I absolutely hated it. I knew that debt was pulling me away from my ideal lifestyle, so it had to go.

Secondly, family legacy is my other "why." This is equal to my first "why." I have always been extremely passionate about the well-being of the Norris family. There is nothing more concerning than leaving a poor legacy behind for my current and future family. My mother and father instilled in me early on the value of family. They taught me firsthand how to be selfless by often putting me and my brothers' needs before theirs. I have carried on this approach to my own family. If you think I was miserable over the past four years while LeAnn and I were becoming debt slayers, you may be right. However, I was fighting for our family legacy. The Norrises will not be known as individuals not reaching their full potential because financial obligations wore them down or defeated them. Our legacy will be very similar to the Lannisters on the popular TV show, Game of Thrones, "A Norris always pays their debt." The financial part of the show, of course.

...

Your "why" may be something totally different. Maybe you want to be debt free so you can travel the world for the next couple of years. Your "why" could be to retire early or become a yoga instructor. Whatever your "why" is, use it to fuel your fire to fight the good fight of becoming a debt slayer! Once you do a little meditation and reflection on what you really want to accomplish in your lifetime, you will be charged to evaporate the debt.
If you can't decide now, use the placeholder of avoiding dying with debt. The average person will die with $61K in debt. Ask yourself, do you really want to leave this baggage behind for your loved ones?

FINANCIAL FREEDOM

By now, you have realized that this book is more about lifestyle than financial advice. The reason is that becoming debt free takes significant lifestyle changes, while not having debt provides a lifestyle of more freedom. Financial freedom is lifestyle freedom that allows one to freely invest his or her time and resources into the things they care about when they care about them. This is an excellent reason to get rid of your debt. When someone has financial freedom, he or she can retire, travel, invest, donate, take a leave from work, and enjoy wealth when and wherever without the anxiety of missing a loan payment or a bill.

This lifestyle of freedom goes beyond the financial rim. A lifestyle of freedom allows a person to focus on the things he or she loves. With this freedom, he or she can hone in on their purpose in life. Fulfilling one's purpose leads to greater satisfaction for living and impacts society, creating a better world as a whole. A better world means happy people, less poverty, and anything else that sounds good. Do you see the correlation of why debt is terrible yet? Here is the formula in the simplest form: Financial freedom = Lifestyle freedom = Freedom to do the things we love when we love and how we love.

HABITS, HABITS, HABITS

Relying on debt cultivates bad habits that impact our lives negatively. For example, we live in a world of instant gratification. Need a car? Call an Uber. Are you hungry? Order from DoorDash. You want your UGG boots today? Click Amazon Prime. Looking for love? Hop on Tinder. While these are all great benefits, the average American over utilizes this instant expectation leading to some horrible financial habits. For instance, when we want an Uber, a nice dinner, or even the UGG boots when we don't have any money, we use our favorite credit card. There's a national outstanding billion-dollar credit card balance for proof. Using credit or loans for instant gratification removes principles like hard work, patience, willpower, and self-reliance from your arsenal, which are the most essential characteristics of successful people quoted by Forbes and Inc. How else does one develop these traits without putting them to good use? Leveraging loans, credit, and cash advances surely do not help.

Tony Robbins says it best, "The secret of success is learning how to use pain and pleasure instead of having pain and pleasure use you." Instant gratification has led eight out of 10 people to let pleasure control them and neglect allowing the pain of not having something to drive positive behavior. If we ignore the urge of instant gratification, we will learn to consistently obtain the things we desire over and over again without DEBT. Having the skill set to achieve your financial goals is much more important than temporary pleasure.

WHAT IS DEBT?

What is debt in the first place? Debt is any amount of money lent to the borrower that must be repaid to the lender. This list includes an unpaid credit card balance, student loan, car loan, business loan, mortgage, home equity line of credit, and a medical bill to name a few. Some debts that may not be as obvious are tax bills owed to the IRS, mobile phone payment plans, bank overdraft charges, interest-free credit cards, payment plans for goods received in advance, and even IOUs (I owe you) to your friends for lunch. The one thing that all of these debts have in common is that they must be repaid, despite the varying contingencies and interest rates on the loans.

Most debts are interest bearing, causing the borrower to pay back a higher amount than the original principal balance. The average American will spend about $280,000 in interest over their lifetime. The goal is to avoid this scenario. The less you pay in interest, the more you save, the more assets you obtain, the more financial freedom, and a better quality of life you are awarded. So run the next time you hear sayings like: "Student loans are good debt. Everyone has debt. Debt is normal. Debt creates opportunities you did not have before. It takes money to make money."

...

HAVING DEBT DOES NOT MAKE YOU A VILLAIN

Now is a good time to clarify that if you have debt, you are not a villain. It is understood that you are educated, competent, financially sound, ambitious, hard-working, smart, and any other positive adjective out there. Having debt does not and should not put you in a derogatory box. In fact, being in debt does not necessarily mean you do not cherish financial freedom or that you suffer from bad habits created by giving in to instant gratification. You are just normal if you have debt.

Debt is a gateway to more debt and can surprisingly lead the smartest, brightest, and most financially sound to a mountain of loans by being normal. Ordinary people go to college on borrowed money, graduate college to purchase a brand-new car that is financed for 60 months, then eventually buy a home that requires payments for a long 30 years. Trust us, we have done it all. However, we realized that "normal" was leading us down a path of high consumption and paying lenders close to hundreds of thousands in interest over our lifetime. Get rid of the debt.

Chapter 10:

FRUGALITY AND BUDGETING

There are two lifestyles that we leaned on to become debt free and will continue to follow to reach financial independence, ultimately providing a more fulfilling life. The first and most pivotal lifestyle required for becoming debt free and building wealth is frugality. According to Google, frugality is the quality of being economical with money or food; thriftiness. That's a broad definition, so here is some clarity. Frugality is the act of spending wisely and intentionally with your money. Living this type of lifestyle requires active management of your finances. Therefore, having a monthly budget is essential. Your budget is the only thing that can validate your expenses and track your month over month spending changes within a category. It's a tool to help you manage your money down to the penny. In addition, frugal people live within or under their means. If you make $1,000 a week, you live on something closer to $400. We will share some of the strategies we used in certain budget categories.

- LeAnn -

As mentioned previously in our story, I admit to being naturally frugal. Frugal is in my personality. I was made fun of by my friends for this noticeable attribute, as early as high school. In college, I distinctly remember one of my classmates calling me "Frugal Franny." Frugality is also in my DNA. Growing up, my parents never passed up taking advantage of a good discount nor clipping coupons. Many people may confuse my frugal lifestyle with cheapness. However, I appreciate nice things like everyone else - traveling, luxury cars, quality food, and fashion to name a few. This is one of the major reasons I have always hated debt and was quite furious at the student loan debt crisis Tim and I found ourselves in. My goal as "Frugal Franny" is to plainly be smart with money. To spend money on things I truly desire. To create intergenerational wealth for my family, while enjoying life doing it. Frugality does not mean you can never casually dine at a fancy restaurant, treat yourself, or travel the world. It's about being intentional with every dollar spent down to the penny. Frugality is living below your means now, to obtain the things you desire later. Deciding where to sacrifice now to be debt free and build wealth in the future, has always been my approach.

CREATE A BUDGET

So how exactly does one start to live a more frugal lifestyle? The first step is creating a budget, a tight one. Before Tim and I really dug deep into our debt, I had a budget, but it was not specific. Each month, I would allocate general dollar amounts to about five categories: Living Expenses/Bills, Loan Payments (minimum), Retirement, Savings and Tithes, and Fun Money. I had an idea of how much I wanted to allocate to each category and I felt responsible in my decisions. I was paying my bills, saving money, and using the rest for traveling, clothes, etc. However, after speaking to my sister, Brittny, she shed light on a class that she was attending with her husband called Financial Peace University by Dave Ramsey. She gave me a copy of the suggested budget sheet recommended in her class. After reviewing the budget template, I realized my budget was nothing more than an organized way to split up my paycheck to fit my lifestyle. The sheet she shared with me broke down my category of living expenses and bills into about 10 categories under one. The budget sheet required that you create an every-dollar budget, knowing exactly how much you will spend that month on rent/mortgage, water bill, gas bill, etc. This budget system demanded you to think about potential upcoming maintenance on your car, doctor appointments, etc., for the month. You have to use your predicted income for the month and think about every possible thing you need or want to spend money on and make a conscious decision regarding how much you want or need to pay. This may sound like a taxing monthly endeavor; however, once you get used to budgeting, it becomes easier and quite fun.

PUSH YOURSELF

When we really got deep into our debt-free journey, we created a stringent budget and allocated the bare minimum amount of funds to each category. You may remember we mentioned only budgeting $25 in our restaurant category. Interesting right? This is the real amount that I budgeted for Tim and me in the restaurant category while we were getting out of debt. No, this didn't buy us much more than a meal from Chick-fil-A, but at least we felt like we could grab that one or two meals when we were on the go and pressed for time. I know a $25/month restaurant budget seems unrealistic for a lot of people. This does not have to be your budget even with a lot of debt. Personally, I'd rather eat at home and set a higher budget in a different category. Tailor your budget to you and your family. Tim actually loves eating out, so we had to really come to a compromise on this aspect of our budget. And yes, now that we are out of debt, our restaurant budget is way more than $25 and allows for nice dinners on a Friday night more than once a month.

STRICT BUDGET

Let's be clear though, when making your budget with the goal of being debt free, you will need to be very strict in many areas. Challenge yourself. Do you really need new clothes? Can you suggest a girls' night-in versus a girls' night-out? Can you start meal prepping instead of going out of the office every day for lunch? As you create your budget, really drill down into each area and see where you can be as economical as possible. Realistically, you will have months with special occasions, holidays, etc. This is OK, just budget for the bare minimum that you will need. Ladies, do you have to get a full set of nails or can you settle with just a polish this time or better yet, paint your nails yourself? Fellas, will anyone really notice if you wear the same blue suit to a different event? Tim and I actually had an inside joke of his "wedding suit." He wore the same old faithful blue suit to multiple weddings and events during our debt-free journey. Hey, it looked good to me every time. Minimalism at its finest. Remember this is only temporary! Well, creating a monthly budget should be something you incorporate into your lifestyle no matter how much is in your bank account but the minimal spending in each category is only temporary. Keep the goal in mind…debt free ASAP!

TAILOR YOUR BUDGETING

Budgeting might be new to you and quite frankly you might not like doing it. It requires thinking, planning, organization, and most importantly, it only works if you stick to the budget plan. To avoid abandoning your much-needed budget, make the task of budgeting a little more enjoyable. Tailor your budgeting system to your personality. For the old-fashioned people, pull out a pen and paper and start creating those categories and crunching numbers with a calculator. Business folks, open an Excel document and start building Excel formulas to populate the budget each month based upon previous months and run the calculations. Millennials, download an app for budgeting and sync it to your bank account. Whatever makes the budget easy and accessible for you will work. The only thing you can do wrong is "blow the budget."

Having cash nowadays is an anomaly. Although credit and debit cards are very convenient, it is easy to swipe away with a card or press "use this payment method" to the card that is saved on your Amazon account. Therefore, when we were getting out of debt, we utilized the cash method or envelope system. After doing the budget, I would go to the bank and pull out the exact amount of cash that was allocated for every category. This made it really simple not to overspend. When grocery shopping at the end of the month, I knew exactly what could be spent based on the remaining money in the cash envelope. There are studies that suggest purchasing with plastic cards is less of an emotional experience than purchasing with cash, causing consumption to increase.

Make budgeting a date night, or if you are single, a time of personal reflection and growth. Discuss or think about your goals financially, giving, travel, etc. Then, set dates and deadlines to achieve those goals. Determine how quickly you can pay off your debt (at minimum) and then imagine your life of financial freedom after your debt is paid. Imagine those vacations, those moments of blessing your family or strangers, and investing. You will be surprised how much motivation you get from dreaming. Oh, and budgeting.

BEAT YOUR BUDGET

One of my favorite parts of budgeting was "beating our budget" for the month. This means that actual expenses were less than forecasted expenses for the month. When Tim and I really got on one accord with the budget, we were able to find money that we didn't realize we had. We were able to throw an extra hundred dollars here and there at the loans that we never thought was possible. Sometimes it took a lot of discipline to stay within the budget that we had agreed upon for a given line item, but we held each other accountable. To stay on one accord, if there was a need to change anything in the budget, we communicated, discussed, and had an open dialogue regarding the changes.

I'll confess that I am the budget nerd and thoroughly enjoy punching the numbers and mapping out the expenses for the month. However, each month I review the budget with Tim and we finalize it together. In the trenches of paying the debt off, you might just find yourself excited to take a challenge and spend less on entertainment and more on paying off debt. Then when you get out of debt, you might just find it exciting to see how much you can save and still pay for that dream vacation, debt free of course.

BUDGETING FOR FOOD

Let's tackle grocery shopping first. While groceries are one of the smaller line items in a typical budget, you can really reduce expenses here if you shop the right way. Many people pass up significant discounts on shopping by avoiding coupon clipping. This is one recipe to lower monthly expenses to increase money used toward your debt. My mother is the queen of saving money when shopping at the grocery store. Hence, this is where I picked up a trick or two. She has her coupons clipped, organized, and/or loaded online for checkout. She consistently tracks the weekly deals at the grocery store and gets pure joy from seeing the grocery bill decrease from $200 to $125. This is pretty impressive and sadly even I am not as savvy with grocery shopping. However, when on the journey to being debt free, you have to participate in some level of coupon clipping like we did. While we did not perform extensive coupon clipping, we would quickly browse the weekly sales. If the grocery or hygiene item was usually on our list, we bought when the price was right. I planned meals around what was on sale and what was already in the pantry that could be used to complete a full meal.

Thankfully, nowadays everything is right at your fingertips on your smartphone and you do not have to go through the local newspaper ads to find coupons and clip them with your scissors. Most coupons are right on an app. I personally use my local grocery store app to check for deals and download coupons that automatically came off at the register. After a while, those "50 cents off" coupons end up being worth your while.

There are a few other basic fundamentals of saving money in the food category. One of the major principles is packing your lunch and eating out less in general. I know this is an absolute struggle for many people. Just try to remember that being in debt is an absolute struggle of a lifestyle and with sacrifice comes reward. Carve out some time each week to prepare your meals. If you have food made and ready, you are less likely to spend that $5 - $10 on a quick grab breakfast, lunch, and/or dinner. Use the strain of preparing meals each week to save on the expense of food as motivation to pay off the loans faster. Obviously, there will be times when it is absolutely necessary to eat out, or well, you just deserve a meal prepared by someone else. Take these opportunities to learn how to order financially savvy. Order water instead of tea, soda, or lemonade. Skip the appetizers and dessert and order the least expensive entree on the menu that still satisfies your palate. Trust me, these small changes in behavior will make a significant difference in your debt-free journey.

BUDGETING FOR HOUSING

Housing is usually the largest line item on the budget so choose where you live wisely. This category will be the anchor of expenses by default. Whether you own or rent, it's recommended that you spend no more than 35% on housing. Having said that, there are many variables that impact housing and cost of living, which may be counterintuitive for your budget. These variables include anything from normal inflation to living in a major city with high demand for apartments and houses. Surely these factors dictate price. Therefore, spend the necessary time reflecting on your short-term and long-term financial goals prior to budgeting your housing. This is why the housing category requires more attention up front before committing to yearly rents or a mortgage.

Knowing that housing is the big ticket on the budget, you must be open-minded to alternatives if you want to cut back here. I would have gladly lived at home with my parents when I was on my debt-free journey. However, Tim and I were recently married, and this was not a plausible option. We decided to move into an apartment. After searching various apartments, we realized just how expensive renting could be for a nice apartment in Atlanta. Ultimately, we had to determine what was important to us and how to compromise. Safety and a nice building were important to us, so we compromised on space and a location. For four and a half years, we lived in a one-bedroom apartment. We even welcomed our newborn into the tiny space of less than 750 sq. ft. I am not a financial advisor by any means, but a good rule of thumb is to live below your means and significantly below your means if you are on the journey to being debt free. A one-bedroom apartment may not be feasible for you and your family, or you may already own a home with a very reasonable mortgage. However, at the end of the day everyone needs shelter. The key is to choose where you live based on financial goals and budget accordingly. Not the other way around.

BUDGETING FOR TRANSPORTATION

Transportation is the last fundamental area to focus on in your budget for two reasons. Owning a vehicle typically requires multiple line items per month that add up quickly. There is car insurance, gas, oil changes, tire rotations and balance, and other general maintenance expenses. Secondly, many vehicle owners have auto loans like we once had, which can be expensive. the average amount borrowed for new vehicles is at a record high of $31,453, while the average household income is $59,039. With the common expenses associated with vehicle ownership and high car notes in mind, make the appropriate changes to your budget to counter this costly category.

For instance, my goal was to keep the 2005 Honda Civic coupe, my parents bought me at age 16, until the wheels fell off. Some people might have been ashamed of keeping the same car for close to 10 years like I did. However, the idea of no car note and reliability brought me great fulfillment. More importantly, it reduced the items on my budget sheet under transportation. Unfortunately, my precious gem was deemed totaled when I got into a fender bender shortly after starting work. I was thankful no one was hurt but devastated that paying a car note was around the corner. I soon purchased a middle of the road car, but not luxury. A few months into having the car, I realized that there was no penalty for paying the auto loan off sooner than the 5-year term and paid it off in a year. Modifying and tracking my budget allowed me to understand how much and how fast this loan could be paid.

...

Budgeting is a way of escaping overspending. It does not mean you are limiting yourself, you are just taking control of your finances and not letting your finances take control of you. It's about planning and not overspending. It's about frugality. Even myself, Frugal Franny, had a lot to learn about budgeting and I am glad I did. Also, finding creative ways to save money in your budget is critical for capturing additional funds to pay debt. Let's face it, you have to eat, you have to have shelter, and you have to have transportation. Saving money requires a little brain power when it comes to fundamentals. Budgeting made a tremendous difference in our debt-free journey and is now a pillar in our lifestyle.

Chapter 11:

MINIMIZE YOUR LIFE

We live in a world where the accumulation of stuff is a sign of success. Just look in any direction in your home, at work, in your car, and you will see a surplus of random items in almost any setting. Ironically, large amounts of meaningless possessions make our lives unsuccessful by eating away our finances, time, clarity, and even freedom. Get rid of the clutter by questioning your belongings.

This way of life is known as minimalism and is the second-most important lifestyle to obtain debt freedom, leading to living a more fulfilling life. Minimalism is the perfect complimentary lifestyle to frugality. If you search minimalism on the internet, you will find results that reference the Western art movement of the early 1960s-1970s, simplified architecture and design, or you might even find some IKEA furniture made with minimal material that looks extremely uncomfortable. There are many definitions out there for minimalism. So let's spare you the trouble. In its simplest form, it is the lifestyle of being conscious of your possessions, requiring constant questioning of the items that do or do not add value to your life. Minimalism dates back thousands of years ago and can be found in Christianity, Buddhism, and Islam. The late Steve Jobs, the former CEO of Apple, practically built the trillion-dollar company on principles of minimalism with his simplistic and pared down approach to product and software design.

Minimalism is the opposite of consumerism, the social movement that encourages the consumption of goods and services beyond reason. Consumerism has plagued the United States for many years, birthing the common saying of "keeping up with the Joneses" coined for purchases based on social status alone. In today's technologically advanced world, consumption is seamless. In 2017, companies spent close to $135 billion on digital marketing in the U.S., as mentioned by Forbes. Due to algorithms, digital marketing, mobile apps, in-app marketing, social media, email, and innovative payment options, it's easier than ever to give into consumption desires. Practicing minimalism will help you counter the temptations.

- Tim -

I have been a minimalist since I could remember. LeAnn often makes fun of how quickly I get rid of personal possessions even when they have significant monetary value. Once I find that one pair of shoes or favorite jacket, I wear it over and over again until the excitement of owning the item depletes to zero. Shortly after, it's posted on eBay or placed in the Goodwill basket. Since I can remember, owning too many items in my personal space has flustered me. Just the sight alone of meaningless junk gave me a headache. Every year, I clean house with my clothes and belongings. Even on my music playlists because the emotional experience from a track made in 2018 is just not the same in 2019 for me.

I continuously ask myself "Do I need this item? When will I need it? Does it make me feel happy or does it cause anxiety?" You won't believe what item gave me the most anxiety. Books. Yes, good old books. Books were the one item I would keep for years. I would start books like many, ultimately to not finish. Every day I would stare at the books laying on my nightstand or shelf and think I am a failure for not finishing, despite the achievements obtained in other areas of my life that caused me to be too busy to read in the first place. As the books stacked, the anxiety rose. I soon realized that the books needed to go out the door with the other possessions. Also, attempting to read multiple books at a time was extremely inefficient, discouraging, and honestly wasteful. Now I buy and read one book at a time and refrain from starting others until the first one is completed. Living a minimalist lifestyle will provide better mental health as it did for my own personal perception of self and offer many other benefits like getting out of debt. Fortunately, minimalism is on the rise in America due to the awakening of consumerism and advocates like The Minimalists.

...

Affordability is what LeAnn and I appreciate most about living a minimalist lifestyle. Practicing minimalism throughout our 48-month journey of paying down debt helped us tremendously. First, we purchased fewer items living this lifestyle. Secondly, we were able to make additional money by getting rid of all the meaningless stuff that was literally collecting dust. We sold everything with a value that did not add value to our lives. Being a minimalist is liberating.

Solely relying on your traditional income source to reach debt freedom does not always cut it - at least not swiftly in most cases. Questioning the existence of your belongings, then selling, will free you from items while generating extra money. This lifestyle of acquiring less and getting rid of things you do not need is a win-win. Remember, the strategy is to throw everything you have at your debt as quickly as possible. Practicing minimalism will help with the inevitable intensity that is needed to slay the debt. When our backs were against the wall, shelling out the majority of our incomes on student loans, we had to sell any and everything. I recommend attempting to sell all your useless belongings to pay the debt collectors. After all, you need every dime you can get. You will be surprised at how much stuff you have that is valuable to others. You will be amazed at what people will buy and for how much. The saying "One man's trash is another man's treasure," is so true in this regard.

There are countless websites we used for selling our crap. And I mean crap. Now I will take this time to personally thank Decluttr.com for buying my old MacBook with a fried hard drive from a wine spill during late night studying in grad school. Ladies and gentlemen allow me to introduce to you Decluttr.com, the website that will buy your technology in any condition. Decluttr is an easy and FREE way to sell mobile phones, computers, and media (CDs, DVDs, games, and books). This is the website for you if a couple of old iPhones or DVDs are lying around the house that will never see the light of day again. The technology can even be broken. Don't ask me what this company does with it. Just plug in a few pieces of information about your item, get an instant valuation, ship for FREE and get paid! Minimize your life by getting rid of the clutter and maximize your focus on things that add value to your life.

- LeAnn -

I know the concept of minimalism may be a hard theory to wrap your head around. Prior to marriage, I never once thought I would be a self-proclaimed minimalist. In fact, I never thought about minimalism, period. Although I am frugal and keep track of how much money I spend, I had about 10 too many pairs of jeans, 15 too many pairs of shoes, and 25 too many shirts. Essentially, I had multiple items in my closet that added zero value to my life. Previously, I would buy clothes that I liked and keep them for years. They would just hang in my closet with the tags on them, sometimes never to be worn. I know you're thinking, "I thought she was frugal?" Well, these clothes were definitely purchased at a great bargain, but the point is that I just plain out did not need the items. A great sale does not always mean buy. After creating a strict budget during our debt-free journey, I did not have the wiggle room to purchase items on a "great sale whim." It was either a necessity or not a necessity.

After making conscious decisions when shopping, regardless of the sale, my next task was to clean out the closet. My main goal was to find items to sell because we were on the debt-free journey. Some stuff in my closet was so outdated, Tim would crack up laughing and yell, "trash!" But there were a few gems in there that sold and everything else was donated. Going through this exercise of cleaning out my closet was liberating. I am a neat and organized person by nature so taking my five blue shirts hung up together, down to the one blue shirt that I actually like and wear, felt refreshing. Cleaning out the closet turned into cleaning out and decluttering every space and storage compartment you can think of. If you ever just want to clear your mind, try decluttering and getting rid of tangible items that do not serve a purpose in your life. Try minimalism.

Ultimately, this lifestyle really gave me a new perspective on material items. I was hanging on to so much stuff for the wrong reasons. One reason I kept clothes, shoes, and other random things around was simply because I had spent money on them. Another reason was because I always thought, "I may need this in the future." A lot of items had sentimental value, "aw, I wore this to prom!" There were so many excuses I made up in my head and honestly, I have not thought twice about any items that I got rid of. Adapting the mindset and ways of a minimalism helped take my frugality to the next level. I've learned to utilize things that I already have at home instead of having three kitchen gadgets that do the same thing or multiple pairs of black loafers. When it's time to trade out or upgrade things, I still look for deals in true frugal fashion. Then I am even more excited to make the purchase, because this time I actually need the item.

PART 3: THE TOOLKIT FOR SLAYING DEBT

Chapter 12:

VIRTUES OF A DEBT SLAYER

In reflection of our debt-free journey there were key virtues that carried us to the end. Being a giver was one of them.

BE A GIVER

Those who are good stewards of money not only eliminate debt, save, and invest, but they give to those in need. Philanthropy has been cited as far back as the fourth century B.C. when Egyptians kings donated money for early-stage hospitals. You still see this kind of generous giving in modern times. Warren Buffett, the prolific investor, gave $2.8 billion to charities in 2017 alone. You may say, easy for him, he's one of the top 10 richest men in the world. Keep in mind that Buffett has pledged a donation of 99% of his wealth to charities at death. Since the beginning of time, the wise have found giving to others important. Yet, it is such a hard virtue for many of us to adopt. Whether in debt or debt free.

It is not by chance that giving is a part of the recipe for being a debt slayer and ultimately for financial success. Giving provides just as many human benefits as it does spiritually. From a practical standpoint, being a giver challenges a person to live on less than 100% of their income. Living on less is hard and requires real discipline. Seventy-eight percent of full-time workers expressed they lived paycheck to paycheck in a 2017 CNBC study. That's 78% of the workers in U.S. living on

100% of their income. If you can't think of a meaningful philanthropic purpose to become a giver yet, do it for the discipline you will obtain in your finances. Commit to a percent and live on the rest. LeAnn and I chose 10% at a minimum. While this was a biblical (Deuteronomy 14:22-26) decision, we felt genuine about this percent and where we were giving our treasures.

- Tim -

However, like many, I personally struggled with giving financially my entire life. Giving through community service comes natural, but not so much the financial part. It was not until 2014, when I committed to consistently tithing 10% of my income to the local church, that my personal economic trajectory became stable to increasingly better. It was something about making a philanthropic and biblical commitment like this and sticking with it that made me feel a sense of fulfillment. I am proud to say that we collectively never missed giving at least 10% of our salaries since starting the road to becoming debt free four years ago. This virtue of giving is one of the reasons why we are debt free today.

Challenging yourself to be disciplined with money is just one of the benefits of giving. To be honest, you should give simply for humanitarian reasons. Americans are extremely privileged, compared to other countries. Yet, we often consume all our resources by living on 100%. I know because I have been there. Some places still lack clean water and basic shelter. Being a giver also forces you to be intentional with your money. It brings forth positive energy toward you as well. God, the universe, or people tend to respond to giving positively. Giving can only help. Whether it's philanthropy, personal development, religion, personal gains, tax write-offs, giving is a crucial virtue for a debt slayer and, more importantly, financial success. As a result, you will need to give intentionally, responsibly, and willingly. Give it a try if you haven't already.

IT'S A MARATHON NOT A SPRINT MENTALITY

It is integral to understand that paying off your debt is only temporary, assuming you slice it aggressively like a debt slayer. You must know that this period of dedicating 100% of your time, energy, and resources to debt repayment will be small, compared to your entire life span. Trust us, this is not a forever thing. As a result, knowing that paying off your debt is a small part of the marathon to financial freedom. You will be back to well-deserved vacations, investing like Warren Buffett, and golfing like Tiger Woods in the near future once the debt is slayed. We would often reflect on the journey throughout our four-year process of paying off debt and think this is a very long time. After getting rid of all our debt, we see the benefits vividly.

REFUSE-TO-LOSE ATTITUDE

Having a refuse-to-lose attitude toward getting out of debt is another crucial virtue. Honestly, this is the only way we had the guts to deplete our emergency fund down to $1,000. An amount that was not even enough to cover one month of expenses. However, with our backs against the wall and a refuse-to-lose mentality, the combination is a force not to be reckoned with. God will respond to this energy, and the debt will be chipped away faster than you think. Having a mindset like this does not just happen. Now, if you are naturally in an intense survival mode and can virtually accomplish any goal you write down, kudos for you. If you are like many people, a significant event has to take place before cutting on survival mode where you will do anything to get out of your current situation. The quickest way to adopt a refuse-to-lose attitude for slaying debt is to blow up the financial bridges to being comfortable. Sacrifice your savings account or sell, sell, sell until the point where your lifestyle has changed to the epitome of frugal. If you do not already have the refuse-to-lose attitude, activate by removing your financial cushions for comfort.

DATA DRIVEN

We live in a highly calculated world where most business decisions are based on some type of data or intel. Our society is currently optimized and managed in a real-time setting with dashboards and KPI's also known Key Performance Indicators. If you don't believe it, just visit the census.gov where you can track the population clock of people being born across the world by the second. It is time we adopt this data-driven approach for our personal finances. *Everydollar.com,* the budget app recommended by Dave Ramsey, allows us to create a monthly budget, track spending, and most importantly make decisions off our financial trends and historicals. Not knocking the paper, but there are substantial benefits from web-based analytic tools that can take your budgeting to the next level. We used this tool every week if not every day to map our way out of debt. Also, we use Personal Capital, a free wealth management tool that allows you track all of your financial accounts from one portal. This tool will automatically analyze your finances and make recommendations. Find tools that help you manage your personal finances and specifically your spending data to more effectively obtain your financial goals.

WILLPOWER - SAY NO NOW TO SAY YES LATER

Becoming a debt slayer is not easy. Having willpower is definitely not easy either, but it is a necessary virtue to development. Saying no to friends and family for outings, trips, dinners, gift exchanges, and anything else that requires you to spend money on a social setting was so hard. It should come as no surprise that we were invited to many engagements over the four years we were digging out of debt. Initially, we gave in to the temptations of fun with friends and family but soon realized that this behavior was holding us back from our daunting financial goal. So we simply started saying no. We were invited to plays, ski trips, concerts, golf outings, and more. Thankfully, we were able to avoid spending thousands, by saying "No." We had developed willpower.

- LeAnn -

WELCOME TO HELP ATTITUDE

Don't run from help, welcome it. We can all learn from one another so ask around for the information and resources you need if you don't have it. We opened our ears and minds to friends, family, co-workers, and financial advisor for tips and resources for getting out of debt.

Also, if you are married, get on a the same plan and help each other out. Tim and I working together toward one goal was extremely effective. Especially for becoming debt free. We recommend combining your finances and financial goals with your spouse. This is only recommended if you are married (for legal reasons). When we first started our journey to becoming debt free, we were attacking our debt in silos. I was making strides on my student loans and Tim was knocking down his credit cards and consumer debt. It was great that we were on the same page about financial freedom as a married couple but now we had to actually work together if we wanted to achieve our family goals. Success and achieving milestones were not as sweet if Tim was still being swallowed by his loans and vice versa. Combining our finances and attacking our debt together allowed us to mature in our marriage, advance our journey to financial freedom faster and more efficiently, and operate as a unit. Two moving with collective effort is better than one, when attacking debt as a family.

GOAL ORIENTED

Obviously, you need to set the goal of being debt free to accomplish it. However, setting the target by itself does not achieve the end result. You need to be goal oriented. The fastest way to becoming debt free is frequently and effectively setting goals that will get you to the final goal. Yes, setting goals requires a basic strategy that should blend steps of getting to the end goal plus keeping you motivated. For example, our overarching financial goal was to pay off $429K odd dollars of debt. We used the debt snowball plan to create smaller goals along the way that were tactical, executable, and motivational. One by one we set, tracked, and crossed out each bill, balance, and loan over four years.

Being able to obtain the short-term wins of paying off individual loans is what kept us motivated. If all we set was one goal of paying off the total tab, we would have been discouraged and defeated before the battle started. If you need some help on becoming goal oriented, check out one of our favorite authors, Grant Cardone, who shares in the 10X Rule specific ways to write your goals. He recommends writing goals as if you have already achieved them. Also, he expresses you should write them daily on paper, so it's fresh on your mind. Regardless of using the debt snowball or writing goals out every day, you must frequently set smaller goals to obtain the big one.

Chapter 13:

THE 30+ SIDE HUSTLES OF A DEBT SLAYER

Finding new sources of income is critical for paying down debt expeditiously. As a result, you will need to identify side hustles. It takes some creativity but it's worth the time investment. If identifying side hustles does not come easy, we encourage you to do a simple exercise. Reflect on how creative you were to obtain the debt in the first place and apply that same imagination and alternative thinking to finding additional income sources. Those credit cards or student loan balances will disappear even faster doing so.

Think about it. Before starting college, you study for the SAT, secure recommendations, and apply for many schools. This is usually a stressful process that takes time and dedication. Just imagine what you can accomplish by using the same amount of time and energy towards getting out of debt. For instance, leveraging your SAT prep skills for a fee, if you are a recent graduate. Or instead of reaching out for letters of recommendation, you ask friends and family for suggestions on ways to save or make money, like clipping coupons, side jobs, etc. If you are an entrepreneur with business loans, apply the same market research and financial analysis you used prior to opening the doors toward pricing strategy and product offerings to generate extra revenue. You get where we are going with this approach. Use every inch of your creativity to help aid you in your debt-free journey.

OK, we know we said this would not be a fluffy book that would merely give philosophical examples of how to get out of debt. In this chapter, we will provide 30-plus ways we made extra cash.

...

First, we sat down together to evaluate our resources. We had computers, cars, extra unused items around the house, and investments.

- LeAnn -

LEVERAGING THE COMPUTER
Before leaving the house to look for extra income, we started with our MacBooks. I signed up for a site called *UserTesting*, where I was able to evaluate websites by providing consumer feedback for a small payment in return. The average job on this site was about $10, and I easily made over $100 casually strolling this site over a few months. The user-testing industry has flourished in recent years, as technology has made it seamless for companies to obtain data points from consumers on product direction, user interface and experience, and quality of a product. Corporations do not like taking a risk on mass producing products unless they know that there is a legitimate demand for the item or consumer appetite in other words. Your insight is valuable and they will pay you for it, as they did with us. Type "user testing" in your Google search when you get a chance and you will see countless options.

In the meantime, Tim signed up for surveys on *Amazon Mechanical Turk*. This website pays significantly less than *UserTesting*, but making $3 in between a commercial break during your favorite show is nice. Also, it adds up over a year. He made about $50 on this site. Although these were minor income sources, anything helped. Over time, those small amounts added up and were a great way to make a little money from your couch or your bed, even when you're tired and drained after work. I will not lie, when you have $400K worth of student loan debt, spending 45 minutes to make $20 does not seem worth it at the moment. Trust us, every dollar adds up and likely on a cold, rainy evening, in the middle of January, $20 from the couch is 45 minutes well spent.

- Tim -

Another website I highly recommend exploring is *Upwork*. *Upwork* is an online marketplace for freelance services. If you have any demanded skills like graphic designing, coding, or writing, you can make some serious dough once you build your client base. Freelancers are earning $1.3 billion annually through this site, according to the CEO's LinkedIn page. The downside to this platform is that the barriers to entry are high due to the global competition. I tried for weeks to offer my data analytics and business strategy skills. However, I found it hard to compete with other freelancers who were willing to do the job for cheaper or had a long track record on *Upwork*. After applying for freelance jobs over a few weeks, I had to tap out and move on to a venture that would bring forth immediate cash for paying off debt. Although this website didn't bring in any additional income for us, I still recommend you give it a try. Check out *Fiverr* as well.

There were a couple of other business ventures we explored that would have brought in a lot of additional income from the convenience of our laptops. However, these ventures required upfront capital and operating expenses with no guarantee that a profit would be made. Getting out of debt as fast as possible requires finding income sources that need little to no upfront expenses rather than going deeper into debt. We considered starting an *Etsy* or *Amazon FBA* business, but we would have been consumed with shepherding a new company with overhead expenses in our budget. This was counterintuitive at the time.

...

- LeAnn -

SELL EVERYTHING WITH VALUE THAT ADDS NO VALUE

Tim is really good at posting and selling items, so this was his arena. I joined in by reflecting on all material things in my life and determining if they were necessary. Have I worn this in the last six months? Is this item useful in my life? Why does this still have the price tag on it? Am I ever going to wear this? I piled everything together, including an old curling iron I never used, and we began selling. Selling random clothes and items on platforms and stores such as *eBay, thredUP, Plato's Closet, Rag-O-Rama, Guitar Center,* and *Amazon*, we were able to make over $500.

eBay gets an award for facilitating the purchase of my curling iron that was collecting dust under the bathroom sink for over four years. The item was so old that we could not find it online anymore. However, the curling iron still sold for over $50. For the effort put into selling an item that virtually had zero value to me, that was amazing.

MAKE MONEY WITH MOBILE APPS

It's safe to assume everybody has a smartphone in this day and age. Smartphones have ultimately provided a platform for useful mobile applications in our everyday lives. There are apps from tracking our fitness activity to learning foreign languages. Yes, we know, this is nothing new. In fact, this is probably considered old. Developers have been working to create an app for anything at this point. There are close to 2.2 million apps on the iOS market, not including the Android market. But before you bicker about mobile app clutter, think about all the opportunities there are to make money in this endless pool of mobile apps at your fingertips. That's what we did.

An app that we downloaded very early in our journey to being debt free was called *Field Agent*. This app is similar to online surveys. You will not make big money, but we managed to make close to $700 over one year. However, it is another source of additional income and it can be fun and convenient. As a "field agent," you are gathering intel and surveying products in actual store locations for various companies. For instance, if a store is running a promotion and they have a display in the store associated with the promotion, you will be required to go to the store, take pictures and answer questions regarding the display. As long as you follow the directions carefully, you have just earned yourself a few extra dollars toward that debt snowball! Cha-ching! Running to local stores and filling out surveys on *Field Agent* eventually became a date night for us. Yes, a date night. OK, well not really a date night per se but we did enjoy spending the time together.

LEVERAGE YOUR VEHICLE WITH MOBILE APPS

Soon we realized that the two vehicles we owned were sadly only used 10% of the time each day. This ironically is the situation for most households. Thanks to the plethora of mobile apps developed for peer-to-peer ridesharing, food delivery, and package delivery, we were able to leverage our cars as a source of income.

For example, Tim used DoorDash, the on-demand food delivery mobile app, to bring in close to $1,500 in about four months. He would hit the streets to make deliveries after his day job that required typical corporate hours 8 a.m. to 5 p.m. Also, he would drive on the weekends. Not only did we use DoorDash as an additional source of income, we also used it as another date night! Tim would drive and deliver the orders while I navigated and kept him company along the way. Intensely working to get out of debt can be very stressful, so making the situation as enjoyable as possible was imperative. The best part of using DoorDash was that we made $1,500 after only spending $20 in total expenses. Since we had the Nissan Leaf, a fully electric vehicle that we charged for free at our apartment building, we only spent $20 on the onboarding with DoorDash for the purchasing card and the T-shirt Tim never wore. That's a return on investment (ROI) of 7,400%. Delivering pizzas was not Tim's first option. However, throwing that $1,500 at our loan balance was more than gratifying. Remember, this is only temporary. Dave Ramsey says it perfectly, "If you live like no one else, later you can live like no one else."

However, if you just cannot stomach delivering pizza, there are many other mobile apps we explored that may be more lucrative and more of your style. There are the obvious Uber and Lyft apps for ridesharing. This is an excellent option if you like meeting and chatting with new people while you earn your extra dollar. Also, if you don't mind a few occasional late-night pukes in your car. Joking, but I hear this does happen more often than not on the late-night shifts.

If you are not feeling delivering pizzas or the unknowing vomit in your car, just rent your vehicle out entirely with Turo. Talk about a way to remove yourself from the equation. This company allows private car owners to rent out their vehicles via an online and mobile interface to anyone who wants to take your ride for a spin. The website currently advertises that you can make up to $1,000 per month. We considered renting out one of our cars, but we are too much of neat freaks. Who were we fooling?

SELL OR DOWNSIZE YOUR VEHICLE

One of the most expensive items you can sell in your household is your car. The average amount borrowed for new vehicles is at a record high of $31,453, while the average household income is $59,039. Cars make up 53% of the average annual household income, before taxes. If you can manage, sell it, buy a beater, and throw the profits at your loans. That's what LeAnn and I did to throw a big chunk of cash at my student loans. We operated out of one car for more than 10 months. While it was tough at times mainly from a convenience standpoint, it paid off immensely. By selling our car, we were able to throw close to $10K at our debt snowball immediately. On the backend, we saved money from eliminating car insurance and maintenance on our second car. I was able to figure out alternatives like public transportation, biking, carpooling, Uber, and Lyft. It was actually much cheaper than the average car note, insurance, and gas that you would pay. Also, I found myself thoroughly enjoying zipping right up the middle of the congested traffic on the train in Atlanta. You cannot beat cheaper, faster, and fewer items to maintain.

Another way to scrap in additional income is to downsize your car. Sell your luxury car, buy a beater, and take the proceeds straight to your loan servicer. We thought about making this move, in the end, to speed up the debt snowball. However, we agreed to keep our nice SUV around to transport our newborn in safety and comfort. This option may be up for grabs for you though!

- LeAnn -

LETTING GO OF NON-RETIREMENT INVESTMENTS AND SAVINGS

This was probably one of the absolute hardest things for me. I am a major saver and always want to ensure that I have enough funds saved up for not one rainy day but at least 10 rainy days. After being introduced to the Dave Ramsey Baby Steps plan and the concept of a $1,000 emergency fund while getting out of debt, I decided to take that leap. I started with my bank account, this was honestly the scariest "submit" button I have ever pressed. I had saved a decent amount of money every month since starting work, for a security blanket. When we got aggressive with our debt and became debt slayers, I closed my eyes and pressed submit to paying every penny above $1,000 toward my student loans. It definitely was not easy, but it was so worth it.

There are probably two types of people out there. There are some who are thinking $1,000 for an emergency fund is more than enough. While there are others who like to prepare for Armageddon, like myself. Again, budgeting and planning are crucial to make sure a non-emergency does not turn into an emergency. For instance, if you know your car is on its last limb and your location/job/life/etc., requires you to have a car, saving to pay for a used car in cash should be in your budget for months. True financial emergencies are unforeseen events that require an immediate financial expenditure. For the person who cannot seem to save $1,000, dig deep into your budget and see where you can cut expenses. Then use some of the suggested creative side hustles to make money listed in this book to bring in extra funds. Lastly, use good ole discipline. Even if financial discipline is not your strong suite initially, set your bank account up to draft a set amount of money out every month and put it into your savings account. I promise you won't even miss it.

As we began to get deeper into the debt-free journey and searching for as many ways as possible to generate additional income, we remembered a few investments that we had. We decided to cash out all our investments outside of existing retirement funds. Again, this may be an arduous task for many and may seem extreme. But just imagine how much you can invest when a large portion of your paycheck is not going toward required debt payments. Make an investment in your personal finances so you can truly make an investment in your life.

- Tim -

CANCEL THE SUBSCRIPTIONS MEMBERSHIPS

Most of us have subscriptions, memberships, and other accounts that charge us monthly for access or service. I know you are thinking, please don't recommend cutting my Xbox live membership. That is correct. Cancel all these accounts, as they will free up more money to throw at your debt snowball. For example, I had a long-standing gym membership at LA Fitness for close to seven years that I canceled. This was a logical decision because there was always a gym at our apartments and my job. We never had cable, so this could not be cut. However, there are millions of Americans who do. This is a big ticket item that will surely save you substantial money. Hulu, Netflix, and Sling TV are all more affordable options if you can't afford to miss your favorite TV shows. For those who have already cut the cable cord, great. Now take it a step further. Cancel your TV subscriptions or piggyback off a friend or relative like we did. We seemed so pathetic to people that my in-laws eventually bought us our own membership to Hulu for Christmas. I kept looking for things to cut and even went as far to cancel my annual subscription to my Microsoft Office to save an epic $6.99 a month. It adds up I promise. I resorted to the Microsoft 2008 software on LeAnn's older MacBook.

ASK FOR MORE HOURS

Not everyone has this option, including myself, but for those who are paid hourly, ask to work more hours. Obtaining more hours at work means larger paychecks. If you work in a retail, restaurant, construction, medical, or legal profession, generally you are in luck. This is one of the easiest ways to bring in more income and it worked for LeAnn. She would work a few extra Saturdays out of the year and it helped us tremendously.

APARTMENT HACKING

We were able to save over $10K by apartment hacking over our debt-free journey. You are probably wondering what's apartment hacking and how we saved over $10K in four years through apartment hacking, right? Well, good news. It was actually simple. If you are willing to move every year, you can typically obtain some really stellar move-in specials from apartments. New apartment buildings love new tenants. So the key is to be a new tenant every year to receive deep discounts. Also, when you move to a new apartment every year, you typically avoid the average annual price increase of 6%. We moved every year since 2014 to see these savings.

SALARY

Last but not least: your salary will typically be the biggest driver of how much and how fast you pay off your debt. As a result, our advice is to be strategic with the jobs you take during your debt-free journey. And by strategic, we mean chose the job that brings home the most money if you have an option to make a higher income.

...

While none of these side hustles to get out of debt mentioned above will make you rich, it will undoubtedly allow you to accumulate thousands, which helps establish an emergency fund of $1,000 and getting the debt snowball rolling.

Lastly, it's understood that by the time we finish writing this chapter, at least one of these companies may go out of business, be acquired, or change its business strategy, etc. However, the point of the matter is to be creative and go find the money. You will likely not win the lotto. Just keep in mind that every dollar adds up.

Chapter 14:

THE DEBT SLAYERS CHECKLIST

After reading through our story, key lifestyles, budgeting and creative side hustles, we know by now you are well on your way to becoming a debt slayer. However, we want to make sure you are left with a detailed guideline to ensure you have the blueprint to debt freedom and living a more fulfilling life. So here is the Debt Slayer Checklist. Following this checklist will set you up for becoming a debt slayer and guide you to debt freedom. Good luck!

Step 1: *DETERMINE YOUR WHY*
The first step for getting out of debt is to determine your why. We challenge you to ponder on the ultimate reason you need your debt to disappear like yesterday. Establish why you want to be debt free and how being debt free will allow you to live a purpose-driven life by accomplishing your personal goals. Ignite the motivation from within and slay the debt!

- ❏ Reflect & Meditate on life goals
- ❏ Dream Session (Think: mental vision board)
- ❏ Establish WHY you want to be debt free
- ❏ Write Down Your Why

Step 2: *RESEARCH YOUR FINANCIAL STATUS*

After determining your why, the second thing you want to figure out when starting your debt-free journey is how much debt you owe. If you are like us in the beginning, you probably have student loans with different servicers, credit cards by multiple providers, and other outstanding bills that might only be visible on your credit reports. It's quite difficult to keep up with principal amount, interest rates, and account information in your head. That's why we recommend spending one to three weeks just researching your debt liabilities. In addition, you will want to determine your financial net worth. Figuring out this basic calculation of Assets - Liabilities (debt) = Net Worth, will be easy once you track down your total debt number. This will allow you to see your financial status "big picture." We recommend a few resources and tools below.

- ❏ Pull FREE Annual Credit Report AnnualCreditReport.com
- ❏ Discover outstanding bills on credit
- ❏ Consider student loan debt consolidation
- ❏ Write/type list of debts with contact information in a spreadsheet
- ❏ Setup online login accounts, if possible, for tracking balances and documentation
- ❏ Gather all your financial information (bank accounts, investments, etc.)
- ❏ Determine/Track net worth
    - ❏ Setup up FREE account with Personal Capital
- ❏ Setup credit monitoring with Credit Karma

Step 3: *WRITE OUT DEBT SNOWBALL*

It's easy to get discouraged while paying off debt so it's all about using psychology to stay motivated on the journey. As a result, we recommend using the debt snowball. The debt snowball was originally made popular by Dave Ramsey and is the debt reduction strategy that consists of paying off debts from smallest to largest balance, while paying the minimum amount on larger debts as you go. We used the debt snowball and obtaining those weekly and monthly wins of paying off loan balances certainly kept us going. Here are three steps to get your debt snowball rolling.

- ❏ Type out debts from smallest to largest in a spreadsheet
- ❏ Update and track the balance on debts as you make payments
- ❏ Print debt snowball list and cross off the debts as you pay!

Step 4: *ESTABLISH MONTHLY BUDGET*

There is only one way to keep up with your money and that's with a budget. Trying to track your monthly purchases in your head does NOT work. Especially, not for getting out of debt. Break out the pen and paper, Excel sheet, and/or app on your smartphone and write down your income and your expenses. You will need to add structure to your finances to become debt free. Having a budget in place will allow you to forecast future expenses, track specific line item expenses, and understand what's left in your budget to pay toward your debt snowball at the end of the month.

- ❏ Consolidate, summarize, and categorize your previous month(s) transactions.
- ❏ Create a budget based on previous months transaction
- ❏ Analyze budget

❑ Find areas to cut back on spending
❑ Create budget with FREE app Everydollar.com

Step 5: ESTABLISH EMERGENCY FUND

To avoid the endless cycle of going back into debt in times of an emergency, you should establish a fund.

❑ Put $1,000 in a savings account
❑ If savings account is above $1,000, pay the amount over $1,000 toward debt

Step 6: MINIMIZE YOUR LIFE

Avoid consumerism. Sell everything in sight. Evaluate anything with a value and confirm that it adds value to your life. If not, sell it. Declutter your space and your mind, by selling items or donating things that are too worn for reselling.

❑ Question all belongings in your house, car, storage for the value it adds to you.
❑ Sell all items that bring you zero value or stress (eBay, Amazon, thrift stores)
❑ Evaluate future purchases based on long-term pleasure

Step 7: CREATE YOUR WAY

Becoming a debt slayer will definitely take creativity, we want to go above and beyond the traditional income. Selling items, releasing investments, downsize your house and/or car if possible, capitalize on your natural skills, utilize your car, computer and phone for sources of additional income. Increase the money coming in and decrease the money going out.

Step 8: *JOIN A COMMUNITY*

❏ Join a community that will support your debt-free goal (i.e. The Cultivate Freedom and Legacy Community)

Step 9: *HACK AWAY AT THE LOANS*

Become a debt slayer by paying off loans. Get rid of the very source that is holding you back from financial freedom.

CONCLUSION

The lifestyles of frugality and minimalism along with intense focus and creativity on paying off loans for the past 48 months was the recipe for us to succeed. However, avoiding debt and paying off debt should not be your life mission. When you focus on something consistently, you become it. Follow this game plan, pay off the debt ASAP, and move on with building wealth and your purpose in life. This will ultimately lead you to a more fulfilling life. That's why you pay off your debt in the first place. Clear the debt to clear your mind. Free yourself mentally and financially from lending institutions to fulfill your purpose in life.

You can bet your bottom dollar that our family will not be focusing on getting out of debt anymore now that we slaughtered a frightening $429K in loans. This book is not to teach people to be "risk-averse," avoid traveling, not to consume pleasures, or to be some type of "no-debt" zombie. Instead, it is to tell our story of how two millennials who worked diligently to achieve a goal that seemed virtually impossible to man and to help inspire others to live a life of financial freedom. Our goal is to encourage a way of life that temporarily focuses on crushing financial burdens to ultimately propel financial gain. We believe that no matter what your income may be or how much debt you have, at any moment in your life, you can make the decision to be financially free. You have what it takes to be disciplined, have willpower, be frugal, and all the attributes of a debt slayer. Dig deep to determine your "why" for becoming debt free. Write that reason or reasons down, meditate on it and start the journey. We truly hope this book has provided some level of inspiration that achieving debt freedom is possible. We look forward to what is in store for your freedom and legacy. You got this!

DEFINITIONS

Apartment Hacking: Moving to new apartment buildings at the end of each lease period to avoid price increases and to get move-in incentives.

Baby Steps Program: 7-Step plan for getting out of debt created by Dave Ramsey.

Beat the Budget: This occurs when your actual expenses are less than your forecasted expenses for the month.

Budgeting: Using your actual or estimated income and predicted expenses to plan and track financial trajectory for a period of time.

Consumerism: The social movement that encourages the consumption of goods and services beyond reason and necessity.

Data Driven: The idea centered around using collected data to accomplish financial goals. In this context, you would use your personal finance data as monthly income and spending statistics to determine your budget.

Debt: Any amount of money lent to the borrower that must be repaid to the lender.

Debt- free: Financial state of not owing anyone or any entity money.

Debt Reduction: Actively decreasing loan balances (and increasing wealth!).

Debt Slayer: An individual who is aggressively paying down debt.

Debt Snowball: Payment strategy where debt is paid off from smallest amount to largest, regardless of associated interest rate. This method was popularized by Dave Ramsey.

Disposable Income: Income minus standard paycheck deductions such as taxes, social security, and other mandated local, state, federal government deductions or elective deductions such as benefits.

Emergency Fund: A fund established exclusively for unexpected spending, intended to avoid going into debt. Emergencies include situations such as a flat tire, unexpected loss of wages, AC unit goes out, etc.

Financial Freedom/Financial Independence: A financial state where the individual no longer has to earn a wage to cover living expenses and can live off their existing investments.

Frugality: The act of spending wisely and intentionally with your money.

Frugal Franny: An individual who makes conscious decisions about their spending habits and where their money goes.

Generational Wealth: Accumulated assets from one generation that will be passed down to the next generation.

Goal-Oriented: Individual that actively plans, sets goals and executes them.

House Hacking: A phrase coined by real-estate investor, Brandon Turner, taking place when a homeowner rents out their home to renters who ultimately pay their mortgage and some.

Instant Gratification: The urgent want for an item that drives someone to go into debt to acquire the item and gain immediate emotional fulfillment.

Legacy: A financial or intellectual gift handed down from one person to another.

Lifestyle Freedom: The ability to live a lifestyle centered around passion rather than focused on income and finances.

Middle-Class Squeeze: Students from middle-class families obtain more student loan debt than peers from lower and higher social classes.

Minimalism: Lifestyle of being conscious of your possessions requiring constant questioning of the items that do not add value to your life.

Nissan Leaf: A fully electric vehicle that was more cost efficient for Tim and LeAnn.

Non-retirement Investments: Assets that do not have restrictions on withdrawal before the retirement age mandated by the government. Non-retirement accounts and assets include brokerage account investments, money market accounts, and real estate.

Side Hustle: Any income earned outside of primary job.

Skills-Gap: Phrase used to describe the gap between individuals who are actively seeking employment but do not have the necessary skills for the open jobs that employers are looking fill.

Slay Debt: The act of reducing debt aggressively.

Student Loan Consolidation: The process of consolidating multiple student loans to obtain a lower interest rate on one loan.

Team Oriented: Working with people to gather and share new ideas on personal finance to achieve financial goals.

Tesla: A fully electric high-performance vehicle that can accelerate 0 – 60mph in 3.2 seconds.

Willpower: The ability to withstand consumerism and stay the course with your financial plan.

RESOURCES

TOOLS

EveryDollar | Budgeting Application
everydollar.com

Personal Capital | Financial Management
Application
personalcapital.com

MEDIA

**"Minimalism: A Documentary About the
Important Things"** | Documentary
netflix.com

The Dave Ramsey Show | Podcast
daveramsey.com/show/podcasts

SCHOLAR

FAFSA | Federal Student Aid
fafsa.ed.gov

MyFedLoan | Student Loan Consolidation
myfedloan.org

OTHER

Cultivate Freedom & Legacy | Blog
cultivatefl.org/blog

LeAnn Norris | Blog & Coaching
www.leannnorris.com

ACKNOWLEDGEMENTS

This book would not be possible without the mentorship, guidance, and help of others. Special thanks to:

Lee Norris Sr. and Theresa Norris for being our biggest cheerleaders on our journey to become debt slayers. Also, for being our weekly, if not daily, motivators and prayer warriors while writing this book. Also, thank you Lee Norris Jr. and Jonathan Norris for your guidance and support for the development of this book.

Phillip Ballentine and Sonya Ballentine for being great parents by showing us the recipe for frugality through example early in life. You all are indeed the discount gurus.

Brittny Frazier for being the caring sister you are. Your willingness to help with open arms has propelled us forward in many ways.

George Cleveland and Antoinette Cleveland for pouring into ongoing mentorship and resources into our family that have directly contributed to this book.

Special thanks to Erika Northington, Terrence Campbell, and Chris McHenry for your generous contributions to this project.

Last but not least, thank you Robert Kallen for exposing me, Tim, to the raw and dismal data of social issues in America and giving us candid feedback throughout this project.

We love and thank you all!

ABOUT THE AUTHORS

Timothy Norris is a native of Atlanta, GA and is currently a procurement manager for a Fortune 500 corporation. He obtained his bachelor's degree in business administration at Morehouse College and received a Master of Economics from DePaul University. Studying economics in graduate school was a wakeup call for Timothy. He realized there were far too many students, like himself, deep in debt with no real action plan. His goal is to help people build a solid financial legacy through Cultivate Freedom and Legacy, the company he and his wife started to help others obtain financial independence to live a more fulfilling life.

LeAnn Norris is a general dentist in her hometown of Atlanta, GA. She was born, raised, and educated in Georgia, obtaining her B.S. degree in chemistry from Spelman College and her Doctor of Dental Medicine from the Dental College of Georgia at Augusta University. She has always been diligent about saving money and hated debt despite finding herself in the massive student loan crisis that has plagued many millennials. LeAnn is passionate about helping others achieve financial freedom through debt elimination. As co-founder of Cultivate Freedom and Legacy, she plays a pivotal role in educating and coaching individuals in pursuit of a debt free life.

Tim and LeAnn have been married for five years and they are the proud parents of their toddler son, Liam.

NOTES

Introduction

1. Dave Ramsey, "How to Get Out of Debt With the Debt Snowball Plan," Daveramsey.com, https://www.daveramsey.com/blog/get-out-of-debt-with-the-debt-snowball-plan (accessed 2019)
2. Josh Mitchell, "Student Debt Is About to Set Another Record, But the Picture Isn't All Bad," wsj.com, May 2, 2016, https://blogs.wsj.com/economics/2016/05/02/student-debt-is-about-to-set-another-record-but-the-picture-isnt-all-bad/ (accessed 2019)
3. James Bessen, "Employers Aren't Just Whining – the "Skills Gap," Is Real" hbr.org, August 25, 2014, https://hbr.org/2014/08/employers-arent-just-whining-the-skills-gap-is-real (accessed 2019)
4. Zack Friedman, "Student Loan Debt Statistics In 2020: A Record $1.6 Trillion," Feb 3, 2020, https://www.forbes.com/sites/zackfriedman/2020/02/03/student-loan-debt-statistics/#616f3623281f, (accessed 2020)
5. Jessica Dickler, "Credit card debt is worse for those with high income," CNBC.com, December 18 2019, https://www.cnbc.com/2019/12/18/credit-card-debt-is-worse-for-those-with-high-income.html (accessed 2019)
6. Kelly Holland, "Eight in 10 Americans are in debt: Study," CNBC.com, July 29 2015, https://www.cnbc.com/2015/07/29/eight-in-10-americans-are-in-debt.html (accessed 2019)
7. Bill Fay, "The Emotional Effects of Debt," debt.org, https://www.debt.org/advice/emotional-effects/ (accessed 2019)

8. IonTuition, "New Survey Shows Student Loan Debt's Impact on Relationships," Iontuition.com, August 2, 2016, https://www.iontuition.com/new-survey-shows-student-loan-debts-impact-relationships/ (accessed 2019)

9. Jessica Dickler, "1 in 8 divorces caused by student loan debt," usatoday.com, August 15, 2018, https://www.usatoday.com/story/money/personalfinance/2018/08/15/student-loan-debt-divorce-rate/987977002/ (accessed 2019)

10. Patrick Ewers, "Want a Happier, More Fulfilling Life? 75-Year Harvard Study Says Focus on This 1 Thing," medium.com, Jan 25, 2018, https://medium.com/the-mission/want-a-happier-more-fulfilling-life-75-year-harvard-study-says-focus-on-this-1-thing-714e22c99ffc (accessed 2019)

11. Farzon A. Nahvi, "I'm a Doctor and Even I Can't Afford My Student Loans," nytimes.com, Aug. 20, 2018, https://www.nytimes.com/2018/08/20/opinion/medical-school-student-loans-tuition-debt-doctor.html (accessed 2019)

PART 1: OUR STORY OF BECOMING DEBT SLAYERS

Chapter 2: The Middle Class Squeeze

1. Michael Stratford, "Study: Student Debt Squeezes Middle Class the Most," insidehighered.com, December 11, 2013, https://www.insidehighered.com/quicktakes/2013/12/11/study-student-debt-squeezes-middle-class-most (accessed 2020)

2. U.S. Department of Education, National Center for Education Statistics, "Digest of Education

Statistics," 2019, https://nces.ed.gov/fastfacts/display.asp?id=76, (accessed 2019)

3. FAFSA, "Complete the FAFSA® Form," https://studentaid.gov/h/apply-for-aid/fafsa

Chapter 3: Instant Gratification

1. Morehouse College, "Tuition Remission HR 500.3:," morehouse.edu, January 1, 2008, https://www.morehouse.edu/media/mcpoliciesand procedures/section5humanresources/TuitionRemi ssionHR500.3.pdf (accessed 2020)
2. Devin O'Brien, "Chicago Rent Prices By Neighborhood This February," zumper.com, March 4, 2015, https://www.zumper.com/blog/2015/03/chicago-rent-prices-by-neighborhood-february-2015/ (accessed 2019)
3. Libertina Brandt, "Here's how much it costs to rent a one-bedroom apartment in 15 major US cities," businessinsider.com, Jul 24, 2019, https://www.businessinsider.com/cost-of-one-bedroom-apartment-rent-major-us-cities-2019-6 (accessed 2019)

4. GFSC, "Eligibility for the HOPE Scholarship," gafutures.org, 2020, https://www.gafutures.org/hope-state-aid-programs/hope-zell-miller-scholarships/hope-scholarship/eligibility (accessed 2020)

Chapter 5: Taking Action

1 Dave Ramsey, "How to Get Out of Debt With the Debt Snowball Plan," Daveramsey.com, https://www.daveramsey.com/blog/get-out-of-debt-with-the-debt-snowball-plan (accessed 2019)

Chapter 6: What happened to our Tesla?

1. Dave Ramsey, "How to Get Out of Debt With the Debt Snowball Plan," Daveramsey.com, https://www.daveramsey.com/blog/get-out-of-debt-with-the-debt-snowball-plan (accessed 2019)

2. Tesla, https://www.tesla.com/model3/design#battery (accessed 2019)

Chapter 7: Consolidating Our Debt

1. Kimber Solana, "ADA-endorsed student loan program rebrands to Laurel Road," ada.org, June 15, 2017, https://www.ada.org/en/publications/ada-news/2017-archive/june/ada-endorsed-student-loan-program-rebrands-to-laurel-road (accessed 2019)

2. FedLoan Servicing, "Ways to Pay," myfedloan.org, 2020, https://myfedloan.org/borrowers/payments-billing/payment-methods/direct-debit (accessed 2019)

Chapter 8: Becoming Debt Slayers

1. Dave Ramsey, "How to Get Out of Debt With the Debt Snowball Plan," Daveramsey.com, https://www.daveramsey.com/blog/get-out-of-debt-with-the-debt-snowball-plan (accessed 2019)

2. Everydollar, "Budgeting Just Got Easy," everydollar.com, 2020, https://www.everydollar.com/app/sign-up/daveramsey?ictid=0D8832667&_ga=2.99254302.1827033806.1585519630-585537414.1585519629 (accessed 2020)

PART 2: LIVING A MORE FULFILLING LIFE

Chapter 9: Why Get Out of Debt?

1. Zack Friedman, "Student Loan Debt Statistics In 2020: A Record $1.6 Trillion," Feb 3, 2020, https://www.forbes.com/sites/zackfriedman/2020/02/03/student-loan-debt-statistics/#616f3623281f, (accessed 2020)

2. NCLC, "Consumer Debt Collection Facts," nclc.org, February 2018, https://www.nclc.org/issues/consumer-debt-collection-facts.html (accessed 2020)

3. GuruFocus, "Household Debt Is Enslaving Americans," Nasdaq.com, May 22, 2017, https://www.nasdaq.com/articles/household-debt-enslaving-americans-2017-05-22 (accessed 2020)

4. Jessica Dickler, "Credit card debt is worse for those with high income," CNBC.com, December 18 2019, https://www.cnbc.com/2019/12/18/credit-card-debt-is-worse-for-those-with-high-income.html (accessed 2019)

5. Kelly Holland, "Eight in 10 Americans are in debt: Study," CNBC.com, July 29 2015, https://www.cnbc.com/2015/07/29/eight-in-10-americans-are-in-debt.html (accessed 2019)

6. Jennifer Calfas, "Americans Have So Much Debt They're Taking It to The Grave," money.com, March 22, 2017, https://money.com/americans-die-in-debt/ (accessed 2019)

7. Tony Robbins, "What Drives Your Decisions," tonyrobbins.com, 2020, https://www.tonyrobbins.com/mind-

meaning/what-drives-your-decisions/ (accessed 2020)

8. Kelly Holland, "Eight in 10 Americans are in debt: Study," cnbc.com, July 29, 2015, https://www.cnbc.com/2015/07/29/eight-in-10-americans-are-in-debt.html (accessed 2019)

9. Quentin Fottrell, "The Average American Pays $280,000 In Interest," marketwatch.com, January 14, 2015, https://www.marketwatch.com/story/the-average-american-pays-280000-in-interest-2015-01-14 (accessed 2019)

10. Dave Ramsey, "Financial Peace University Member Workbook," Hardcover, 2019 (accessed 2020)

11. Phil LeBeau, "A $523 Monthly Payment Is the New

12. Standard for Car Buyers," cnbc.com, May 31, 2018, https://www.cnbc.com/2018/05/31/a-523-monthly-payment-is-the-new-standard-for-car-buyers.html (accessed 2019)

13. US Census Bureau, "Was median household income in 2016 the highest median household income ever reported from the Current Population Survey Annual Social and Economic Supplement?" census.org, September 17, 2017, https://www.census.gov/newsroom/blogs/random-samplings/2017/09/was_median_household.html (accessed 2019)

14. Taehoon Kim, ""Extreme minimalism" - iPhone Design Philosophy in a word," medium.com, June 11, 2016, https://medium.com/@taehoonkim_22222/extrem

e-minimalism-iphone-design-philosophy-in-a-word-63c7b29ae497 (accessed 2020)

Chapter 11: Minimize Your Life

1. Kathleen Chaykowski, "Digital Video Marketing Is A \$135 Billion Industry In The U.S. Alone, Study Finds," forbes.com, October 18 2017, https://www.forbes.com/sites/kathleenchaykowski/2017/10/18/digital-video-marketing-is-a-135-billion-industry-in-the-u-s-alone-study-finds/#432a6449d4dd (accessed 2019)

2. Joshua Fields Millburn & Ryan Nicodemus , The Minimalists, theminimalists.com

PART 3: THE TOOLKIT FOR SLAYING DEBT

Chapter 12: Virtues of a Debt Slayer

1. Jonathan Chew, "Warren Buffett donates \$2.8 billion … again," fortune.com, July 6, 2015, https://fortune.com/2015/07/06/warren-buffett-donation/ (accessed 2020)

2. Jessica Dickler, "Most Americans live paycheck to paycheck," cnbc.com, August 24, 2017, https://www.cnbc.com/2017/08/24/most-americans-live-paycheck-to-paycheck.html (accessed 2019)

3. Everydollar, "Budgeting Just Got Easy," everydollar.com, 2020, https://www.everydollar.com/app/sign-up/daveramsey?ictid=0D8832667&_ga=2.99254302.1827033806.1585519630-585537414.1585519629 (accessed 2020)

4. Grant Cardone, "The 10X Rule: The Only Difference Between Success and Failure," Hardcover, April 26, 2011, (accessed 2020)

Chapter 13: The 30+ Side Hustles of a Debt Slayer

1. Ian Blair, "Mobile App Download and Usage Statistics," buildfire.com, 2020, https://buildfire.com/app-statistics/ (accessed 2020)

2. Standard for Car Buyers," cnbc.com, May 31, 2018, https://www.cnbc.com/2018/05/31/a-523-monthly-payment-is-the-new-standard-for-car-buyers.html (accessed 2019)

3. US Census Bureau, "Was median household income in 2016 the highest median household income ever reported from the Current Population Survey Annual Social and Economic Supplement?" census.org, September 17,

4. 2017, https://www.census.gov/newsroom/blogs/random-samplings/2017/09/was_median_household.html (accessed 2019)

5. Dave Ramsey, "The Total Money Makeover: A Proven Plan for Financial Fitness," Hardcover, December 29, 2009, (accessed 2019)

THE DEBT SLAYERS

THE DEBT SLAYER JOURNAL

The next pages offer guided notes to help you get started on your debt slaying journey. These guided notes pair well with The Debt Slayers Checklist. We are excited for you to become a debt slayer! Good Luck!

-Tim and LeAnn

DETERMINE YOUR WHY

BRAINSTORM + MEDITATE + DREAM

RESEARCH YOUR FINANCIAL STATE

TAKE NOTES ON ANYTHING YOU DISCOVER ON YOUR CREDIT + ACCOUNTS

DETERMINE ALL DEBTS

RESEARCH YOUR
FINANCIAL STATE

TAKE NOTES ON ANYTHING YOU DISCOVER ON YOUR
CREDIT + ACCOUNTS

DETERMINE ALL DEBTS

WRITE OUT DEBT SNOWBALL

STUDENT LOANS + CREDIT CARDS + IOU's +CAR LOANS

SMALLEST

LARGEST

BUDGETING NOTES

JOT DOWN ALL YOUR RECURRING MONTHLY
EXPENSES + INCOME

ESTABLISH EMERGENCY FUND

BRAINSTORM IDEAS ON WAYS TO BUILD THIS FUND.

ARE THERE ANY AREAS YOU CAN CUT FROM YOUR BUDGET?

ARE THERE THINGS YOU CAN DO TO MAKE ADDITIONAL MONEY?

MINIMIZE YOUR LIFE

THINK ABOUT THINGS TO SELL AND GIVE AWAY

CREATE YOUR
WAY OUT OF DEBT

WHAT ARE SOME WAYS YOU CAN BE CREATIVE TO ACHIEVE YOUR DEBT FREE GOAL?

CAR POOLING
MEAL PREP
DOG WALKING

JOIN A COMMUNITY

FIND RESOURCES THAT MOTIVATE & GUIDE YOU TO YOUR DEBT FREE GOAL

1. THEDEBTSLAYERS.COM
2. LEANNNORRIS.COM
3.
4.
5.
6.
7.
8.
9.
10.

SLAY DEBT!

For additional information about The Debt Slayers products and services please contact:

Cultivate Freedom and Legacy, LLC

Email: info@cultivatefl.org

Website: cultivatefl.org

Made in USA - Crawfordsville, IN
51794_9780578498713
12.21.2020 1824